R.U.R.

Over fifty years have passed since Karel Čapek pondered the question of the dehumanizing impact of technological progress upon mankind and expressed his views through the medium of a startling play. But surely it must be only yesterday that he spoke, for the problems he posed in his society of robots are even more pertinent and demanding of solution in an age of computers, space voyages, and automation. R.U.R. *speaks of the way it is now—and casts fearful shadows upon the way it may be, if we cannot mold a better society.*

This is an
Enriched Edition of *R.U.R.*
A Reader's Supplement has been added to the text and includes Biographical and Historical Background, Features of the Author's Style, Character Analysis, and Critical Excerpts. The material was prepared by an editorial committee directed by Harry Shefter, Professor of English, New York University. The contributing editor to this edition was Oscar H. Fidell, educator, writer, and critic.

Titles available in
ENRICHED EDITIONS

R. U. R.

by

Karel Čapek

*Translated from the Czech
by P. Selver and adapted for
the English stage by Nigel Playfair*

edited by
Harry Shefter

WASHINGTON SQUARE PRESS
POCKET BOOKS • NEW YORK

R. U. R.

WASHINGTON SQUARE PRESS edition published June, 1973

2nd printing......................October, 1973

Originally published in English by Oxford University Press in 1923.

L

Published by
POCKET BOOKS, a division of Simon & Schuster, Inc.,
630 Fifth Avenue, New York, N.Y.

WASHINGTON SQUARE PRESS editions are distributed
in the U.S. by Simon & Schuster, Inc., 630 Fifth Avenue,
New York, N.Y. 10020 and in Canada by Simon & Schuster of Canada, Ltd., Richmond Hill, Ontario, Canada.

Standard Book Number: 671-46605-4.

SCENES

CHARACTERS

HARRY DOMAIN, *General Manager for Rossum's Universal Robots*

FABRY, *Chief Engineer for R. U. R.*

DR. GALL, *Head of the Physiological Department, R. U. R.*

DR. HELMAN, *Psychologist-in-Chief*

JACOB BERMAN, *Managing Director, R. U. R.*

ALQUIST, *Clerk of the Works, R. U. R.*

HELENA GLORY, *Daughter of Professor Glory, of Oxbridge University*

EMMA, *Her Maid*

MARIUS, *A Robot*

SULLA, *A Robotess*

RADIUS, *A Robot*

PRIMUS, *A Robot*

HELENA, *A Robotess*

A ROBOT SERVANT and numerous Robots
ON A REMOTE ISLAND

R. U. R.

ACT I

ACT I

‖‖

Central office of the factory of ROSSUM'S UNIVER-
SAL ROBOTS. *Entrance at the back on the right. The
windows look out on to endless rows of factory
buildings.* DOMAIN *is sitting in a revolving chair
at a large "knee-hole" writing table on which stand
an electric lamp, telephone, letter-weight, corres-
pondence file, etc. On the left-hand wall hang large
maps showing steamship and railway routes, a
large calendar, and a clock indicating a few minutes before noon. On the right-hand wall are fas-
tened printed placards:* "CHEAP LABOR. ROSSUM'S
ROBOTS." "ROBOTS FOR THE TROPICS. 150 DOLLARS
EACH." "EVERYONE SHOULD BUY HIS OWN ROBOT." "DO
YOU WANT TO CHEAPEN YOUR OUTPUT? ORDER ROS-
SUM'S ROBOTS": *more maps, shipping transport ar-
rangements, etc. A tape machine showing rates of
exchange stands in one corner. In contrast to these
wall fittings, the floor is covered with a splendid
Turkey carpet. On the right stand a round table, a
sofa, leather armchair, and a bookshelf contain-
ing bottles of wine and spirits instead of books.
Cashier's desk on the left. Next to* DOMAIN'S *table*
SULLA *is typing letters.*

DOMAIN. (*Dictating*) "We do not accept any liability for goods damaged in transit. When the consignment was shipped, we drew your Captain's attention to the fact that the vessel was unsuitable for the transport of Robots. The matter is one for your own Insurance Company. We beg to remain, for Rossum's Universal Robots——" Finished?

SULLA. Yes.

DOMAIN. Another letter. "To the E. B. Hudson Agency, New York. Date. We beg to acknowledge receipt of order for five thousand Robots. As you are sending your own vessel, please dispatch as cargo briquettes for R.U.R., the same to be credited as part-payment of the amount due to us. We beg to remain——" Finished?

SULLA. (*Typing the last word*) Yes.

DOMAIN. "Friedrichswerke, Hamburg. Date. We beg to acknowledge receipt of order for fifteen thousand Robots."

(*The house telephone rings.* DOMAIN *picks it up and speaks into it*)

Hallo, this is the central office—yes—certainly. Oh, yes, as usual. Of course, send them a cable. Good. (*Hangs up the telephone*) Where did I leave off?

SULLA. We beg to acknowledge receipt of order for fifteen thousand R.

DOMAIN. (*Thoughtfully*) Fifteen thousand R. Fifteen thousand R.

MARIUS. (*Entering*) There's a lady, sir, asking to——

DOMAIN. Who is she?

MARIUS. I don't know, sir. She gave me this card.

DOMAIN. (*Reads*) Professor William Glory, St. Trydeswyde's, Oxbridge—Ask her to come in.

MARIUS. (*Opening the door*) Please step this way, ma'am.

Enter HELENA GLORY

(*Exit* MARIUS

DOMAIN. (*Standing up*) What can I do for you, madame?

HELENA. You are Mr. Domain, the general manager.

DOMAIN. I am.

HELENA. I have come to you——

DOMAIN. With Professor Glory's card. That is sufficient.

HELENA. Professor Glory is my father. I am Helena Glory.

DOMAIN. Miss Glory, it is an unusual honor for us—to be—to be——

HELENA. Yes—well.

DOMAIN. To be allowed to welcome the distinguished Professor's daughter. Please sit down. Sulla, you may go. (*Exit* SULLA (*Sitting down*) How can I be of service to you, Miss Glory?

HELENA. I have come here——

DOMAIN. To have a look at our factory where people are made. Like all visitors. Well, there's no objection.

HELENA. I thought it was forbidden——

DOMAIN. It is forbidden to enter the factory, of course. But everybody comes here with an introduction and then——

HELENA. And you show everybody——?

DOMAIN. Only certain things. The manufacture of artificial people is a secret process.

HELENA. If you only knew how enormously that——

DOMAIN. Interests me, you were going to say. Europe's talking about nothing else.

HELENA. Why don't you let me finish speaking?

DOMAIN. I beg your pardon. Did you want to say anything else?

HELENA. I only wanted to ask——

DOMAIN. Whether I could make a special exception in your case and show you our factory. Certainly, Miss Glory.

HELENA. How do you know that I wanted to ask you that?

DOMAIN. They all do. (*Standing up*) We shall consider it a special honor to show you more than the rest, because—indeed—I mean——

HELENA. Thank you.

DOMAIN. But you must undertake not to divulge the least——

HELENA. (*Standing up and giving him her hand*) My word of honor.

DOMAIN. Thank you. Won't you raise your veil?

HELENA. Oh, of course, you want to see me. I beg your pardon.

DOMAIN. What is it, please?

HELENA. Would you mind letting my hand go.

DOMAIN. (*Releasing it*) I beg your pardon.

HELENA. (*Taking off her veil*) You want to see whether I am a spy or not. How cautious you are!

DOMAIN. (*Looking at her intently*) H'm, of course—we—that is——

HELENA. You don't trust me?

DOMAIN. Oh, indeed, Miss Glory, I'm only too delighted. Weren't you lonely on the voyage?

HELENA. Why?

DOMAIN. Because—I mean to say—you're so young.

HELENA. Yes. Shall we go straight into the factory?

DOMAIN. Twenty-two, I think, eh?

HELENA. Twenty-two what?

DOMAIN. Years.

HELENA. Twenty-one. Why do you want to know?

DOMAIN. Because—as—(*With enthusiasm*) You'll make a long stay, won't you?

HELENA. That depends on how much of the factory you show me.

DOMAIN. Oh, hang the factory. But you shall see everything, Miss Glory, indeed you shall. Please sit down. Would you like to hear the story of the invention?

HELENA. Yes, please. (*Sits down.*)

DOMAIN. Well, then. (*Sits down on the writing-table, looks at* HELENA *with rapture, and reels off rapidly*) It was in the year 1922 that old Rossum the great physiologist, who was then quite a young scientist, betook himself to this distant island for the purpose of studying the ocean fauna, full stop. On this occasion he attempted by chemical synthesis to imitate the living matter known as protoplasm, until he suddenly discovered a substance which behaved exactly like living matter, although its chemical composition was different; that was in the year 1932, exactly four hundred years after the discovery of America, whew!

HELENA. Do you know that by heart?

DOMAIN. Yes. Physiology, Miss Glory, is not my line. Shall I go on?

HELENA. Please do.

DOMAIN. (*Solemnly*) And then, Miss Glory, old Rossum wrote the following in his day book: "Nature has found only one method of organizing living matter. There is, however, another method more simple, flexible, and rapid, which has not yet occurred to nature at all. This second process by which life can be developed was discovered by me today." Imagine him, Miss Glory, writing those wonderful words. Imagine him sitting over a test tube and thinking how the whole tree of life would grow from it, how all animals would proceed from it, beginning with some sort of beetle and ending with man himself. A man of different substance from ours. Miss Glory, that was a tremendous moment.

HELENA. Go on, please.

DOMAIN. Now the thing was, how to get the life out of the test tube and hasten development: to form organs, bones and nerves, and so on: to find such substances as catalytics, enzymes, hormones, and so forth, in short—you understand?

HELENA. I don't know. Not much, I'm afraid.

DOMAIN. Never mind. You see, with the help of his tinctures he could make whatever he wanted. He could have produced a Medusa with the brain of a Socrates or a worm fifty yards long. But being without a grain of humor, he took it into his head to make a normal vertebrate. This artificial living matter of his had a raging thirst for life. It didn't mind being sewn up or mixed together. *That*, you'll admit, couldn't be done with natural albumen. And that's how he set about it.

HELENA. About what?

DOMAIN. About imitating nature. First of all he tried making an artificial dog. That took him several years and resulted in a sort of stunted calf which died in a few days. I'll show it you in the museum. And then old Rossum started on the manufacture of man. (*Pause*

HELENA. And I must divulge this to nobody?

DOMAIN. To nobody in the world.

HELENA. It's a pity that it can already be found in every school lesson book.

DOMAIN. Yes. (*Jumps up from the table and sits down beside* HELENA) But do you know what isn't in the lesson books? (*Taps his forehead*) That old Rossum was quite mad. Seriously, Miss Glory, you must keep this to yourself. The old crank actually wanted to make people.

HELENA. But you do make people.

DOMAIN. Synthetically, Miss Helena. But old Rossum meant it actually. He wanted to become a sort of scientific substitute for God, you know. He was a fearful materialist, and that's why he did it all. His sole purpose was nothing more or less than to supply proof that Providence was no longer necessary. So he took it into his head to make people exactly like us. Do you know anything about anatomy?

HELENA. Only a very little.

DOMAIN. So do I. Imagine then that he decided to manufacture everything as in the human body. I'll show you in the museum the bungling attempt it took him ten years to produce. It was to have been a man, but it lived for three days only. Then up came young Rossum, an engineer, the nephew of old Rossum. A wonderful fellow, Miss Glory. When he saw what a mess of it the old man was making, he said: "It's absurd to spend ten years making a man. If you can't make him quicker than nature, you may as well shut up shop." Then he set about learning anatomy himself.

HELENA. There's nothing about that in the lesson books.

DOMAIN. (*Standing up*) The lesson books are full of paid advertisement, and rubbish at that. For example, it says there that the Robots were invented by an old man. But it was young Rossum who had the idea of making living and intelligent working machines. What the lesson books say about the united efforts of the two great Rossums is all a fairy tale. They used to have dreadful rows. The old atheist hadn't the slightest conception of industrial matters, and the end of it was that young Rossum shut him up in some laboratory or other and let him fritter the time away with his monstrosities, while he himself started on the business from an engineer's point of view. Old Rossum cursed him, and before he died he managed to botch up two physiological horrors. Then one day they found him dead in the laboratory. That's the whole story.

HELENA. And what about the young man?

DOMAIN. Well, any one who's looked into anatomy will have seen at once that man is too complicated, and that a good engineer could make him more simply. So young Rossum began to overhaul anatomy and tried to see what could be left out or simplified. In short—but this isn't boring you, Miss Glory?

HELENA. No; on the contrary, it's awfully interesting.

DOMAIN. So young Rossum said to himself: A man is something that, for instance, feels happy, plays the fiddle, likes going for walks, and, in fact, wants to do a whole lot of things that are really unnecessary.

HELENA. Oh!

DOMAIN. Wait a bit. That are unnecessary when he's wanted, let us say, to weave or to count. Do you play the fiddle?

HELENA. No.

DOMAIN. That's a pity. But a working machine must not want to play the fiddle, must not feel happy, must not do a whole lot of other things. A petrol motor must not have tassels or ornaments, Miss Glory. And to manufacture artificial workers is the same thing as to manufacture motors. The process must be of the simplest, and the product of the best from a practical point of view. What sort of worker do you think is the best from a practical point of view?

HELENA. The best? Perhaps the one who is most honest and hard-working.

DOMAIN. No, the cheapest. The one whose needs

are the smallest. Young Rossum invented a worker
with the minimum amount of requirements. He
had to simplify him. He rejected everything that
did not contribute directly to the progress of
work. In this way he rejected everything that
makes man more expensive. In fact, he rejected
man and made the Robot. My dear Miss Glory, the
Robots are not people. Mechanically they are more
perfect than we are, they have an enormously
developed intelligence, but they have no soul.
Have you ever seen what a Robot looks like inside?

HELENA. Good gracious, no!

DOMAIN. Very neat, very simple. Really a beautiful piece of work. Not much in it, but everything
in flawless order. The product of an engineer is
technically at a higher pitch of perfection than a
product of nature.

HELENA. Man is supposed to be the product of
nature.

DOMAIN. So much the worse. Nature hasn't the
least notion of modern engineering. Would you
believe that young Rossum played at being nature?

HELENA. What do you mean?

DOMAIN. He began to manufacture Super-Ro-
bots—regular giants. He tried to make them four
yards high. But they were a frost.

HELENA. A frost?

DOMAIN. Yes. For no reason at all their limbs
used to keep snapping off. Evidently our planet
is too small for giants. Now we only make Robots
of normal size and of very high-class human finish.

HELENA. I saw the first Robots at home. The

town council bought them—I mean engaged them for work.

DOMAIN. Bought them, dear Miss Glory. Robots are bought and sold.

HELENA. These were employed as sweepers. I saw them sweeping. They are so strange and quiet.

DOMAIN. Did you see my typist?

HELENA. I didn't notice her particularly.

DOMAIN. (*Rings*) You see, Rossum's Universal Robot factory don't produce a uniform brand of Robots. We have Robots of finer and coarser grades. The best will live about twenty years.

HELENA. Then they perish?

DOMAIN. Yes, they get used up.

Enter SULLA

DOMAIN. Sulla, let Miss Glory look at you.

HELENA. (*Standing up and holding out her hand*) So glad to meet you. You must feel terribly dull in this out-of-the-way spot, don't you?

SULLA. I don't know, Miss Glory. Please sit down.

HELENA. (*Sitting down*) Where do you come from?

SULLA. From there, from the factory.

HELENA. Ah, you were born there.

SULLA. Yes, I was made there.

HELENA. (*Jumping up*) What?

DOMAIN. (*Laughing*) Sulla is a Robot.

HELENA. Oh, I beg your pardon——

DOMAIN. (*Laying his hand on* SULLA's *shoulder*) Sulla isn't angry. See, Miss Glory, the kind of skin we make. Feel her face.

HELENA. Oh, no, no.

DOMAIN. You wouldn't know that she's of different material from us. Turn round, Sulla.

HELENA. Stop, stop!

DOMAIN. Talk to Miss Glory, Sulla. She's an important visitor.

SULLA. Please sit down. (*Both sit down*) Did you have a pleasant crossing?

HELENA. Oh, yes, certainly.

SULLA. Don't go back on the *Amelia,* Miss Glory. The barometer is falling steadily. Wait for the *Pennsylvania.* That's a very good powerful vessel.

DOMAIN. What's its speed?

SULLA. Twenty knots an hour. Twelve thousand tons. One of the latest vessels, Miss Glory.

HELENA. Tha—thank you.

SULLA. A crew of eighty, Captain Harpy, eight boilers——

DOMAIN. (*Laughing*) That's enough, Sulla. Now show us your knowledge of French.

HELENA. You know French?

SULLA. I know four languages. I can write: Dear Sir, Monsieur, Geehrter Herr, Y Mustre Señor.

HELENA. (*Jumping up*) What nonsense! Sulla isn't a Robot. Sulla is a girl like me. Sulla, it's naughty of you—why do you take part in such a hoax?

SULLA. I am a Robot.

HELENA. No, no, you're not telling the truth. Oh, Sulla, forgive me, I know—they've forced you to do it for an advertisement. Sulla, you are a girl like me, aren't you? Tell me, now.

DOMAIN. I'm sorry, Miss Glory. Sulla is a Robot.

HELENA. *You're* not telling the truth.

DOMAIN. (*Starting up*) What? (*Rings*) Excuse me, Miss Glory, then I must convince you.

Enter MARIUS

DOMAIN. Marius, take Sulla into the testing room for them to open her. Quickly.

HELENA. Where?

DOMAIN. Into the testing room. When they've cut her up, you can go and have a look.

HELENA. I shan't go.

DOMAIN. Excuse me, you spoke of lies.

HELENA. You wouldn't have her killed?

DOMAIN. You can't kill machines.

HELENA. (*Embracing* SULLA) Don't be afraid, Sulla, I won't let you go. Tell me, darling, are they always so cruel to you? You mustn't put up with that, Sulla. You mustn't.

SULLA. I am a Robot.

HELENA. That doesn't matter. Robots are just as good as we are. Sulla, you wouldn't let yourself be cut to pieces.

SULLA. Yes.

HELENA. Oh, you're not afraid of death, then?

SULLA. I cannot tell, Miss Glory.

HELENA. Do you know what would happen to you there?

SULLA. Yes, I should cease to move.

HELENA. How dreadful.

DOMAIN. Marius, tell Miss Glory what you are.

MARIUS. Marius, the Robot.

DOMAIN. Would you take Sulla into the testing room?

MARIUS. Yes.

DOMAIN. Would you be sorry for her?

MARIUS. I cannot tell.

DOMAIN. What would happen to her?

MARIUS. She would cease to move. They would put her into the stamping-mill.

DOMAIN. That is death, Marius. Aren't you afraid of death?

MARIUS. No.

DOMAIN. You see, Miss Glory, the Robots are not attached to life. They have no reason to be. They have no enjoyments. They are less than so much grass.

HELENA. Oh, stop. Send them away.

DOMAIN. Marius, Sulla, you may go.

(*Exeunt* SULLA *and* MARIUS

HELENA. How terrible. It's scandalous!

DOMAIN. Why scandalous?

HELENA. It is, of course it is. Why did you call her Sulla?

DOMAIN. Isn't it a nice name?

HELENA. It's a man's name. Sulla was a Roman General.

DOMAIN. Oh, we thought that Marius and Sulla were lovers.

HELENA. No. Marius and Sulla were generals, and fought against each other in the year—I've forgotten now.

DOMAIN. Come here to the window. What do you see?

HELENA. Bricklayers.

DOMAIN. They are Robots. All our workpeople are Robots. And down there, can you see anything.

HELENA. Some sort of office.

DOMAIN. A counting-house. And in it——

HELENA. Clerks—a lot of clerks.

DOMAIN. They are Robots. All our clerks are Robots. When you see the factory——

(*Sound of factory whistles and sirens*

Midday. The Robots don't know when to stop work. In two hours I'll show you the kneading-trough.

HELENA. What kneading-trough?

DOMAIN. (*Dryly*) The pestles and mortar as it were for beating up the paste. In each one we mix the ingredients for a thousand Robots at one operation. Then there are the vats for the preparation of liver, brains, and so on. Then you'll see the bone factory. After that I'll show you the spinning-mill.

HELENA. What spinning-mill?

DOMAIN. For weaving nerves and veins. Miles and miles of digestive tubes pass through it at a stretch. Then there's the fitting-shed, where all the parts are put together, like motorcars. Next comes the drying-kiln and the warehouse in which the new products work.

HELENA. Good gracious, do they have to work immediately?

DOMAIN. Well, you see, they work like any new appliance. They get used to existence. They sort of grow firm inside. We have to make a slight allowance for natural development. And in the meantime they undergo training.

HELENA. How is that done?

DOMAIN. It's much the same as going to school. They learn to speak, write, and count. They've astonishing memories, you know. If you were to read a twenty-volume encyclopaedia to them, they'd repeat it all to you with absolute accuracy. But they never think of anything new. Then they're sorted out and distributed. Fifteen thousand daily, not counting a regular percentage of defective specimens which are thrown into the stamping-mill . . . and so on—and so on. Oh, let's talk about something else. There's only a handful of us among a hundred thousand Robots, and not one woman. We talk about nothing but the factory, all day, every day. It's just as if we're under a curse, Miss Glory.

HELENA. I'm so sorry I said that—that—you weren't speaking the truth.

(*A knock at the door*

DOMAIN. Come in, boys.

(*From the L. enter* MR. FABRY, DR. GALL, DR. HELMAN, ALQUIST)

DR. GALL. I beg your pardon, I hope we're not in the way.

DOMAIN. Come along in. Miss Glory, here are Mr. Alquist, Mr. Fabry, Dr. Gall, and Dr. Helman. This is Professor Glory's daughter.

HELENA. (*Embarrassed*) How do you do?

FABRY. We had no idea——

DR. GALL. Very honored, I'm sure——

ALQUIST. Welcome, Miss Glory.

(BERMAN *rushes in from the R.*)

BERMAN. Hallo, what's up?

DOMAIN. Come in, Berman. This is Mr. Berman, Miss Glory. This is the daughter of Professor Glory.

HELENA. I'm very glad to meet you.

BERMAN. By Jove, that's splendid. Miss Glory,

may we send a cablegram to the papers about your——

HELENA. No, no, please don't.

DOMAIN. Sit down, please, Miss Glory.

BERMAN. Allow me——

DR. GALL. (*Dragging up armchairs*) Please——

FABRY. Excuse me——

ALQUIST. What sort of a crossing did you have?

DR. GALL. Are you going to stay here long?

FABRY. What do you think of the factory, Miss Glory?

HELMAN. Did you come over on the *Amelia*?

DOMAIN. Be quiet, let Miss Glory speak.

HELENA. (*To* DOMAIN) What am I to speak to them about?

DOMAIN. (*Surprised*) About what you like.

HELENA. Shall . . . may I speak quite frankly?

DOMAIN. Why, of course.

HELENA. (*Wavering, then with desperate resolution*) Tell me, doesn't it ever distress you to be treated like this?

FABRY. Treated?—Who by?

HELENA. Everybody.

(*All look at each other in consternation*)

ALQUIST. Treated?

DR. GALL. What makes you think that?

HELMAN. Treated?

BERMAN. Really!

HELENA. Don't you feel that you might be living a better life?

DR. GALL. Well, that depends what you mean, Miss Glory.

HELENA. I mean that—(*Bursting out*) that it's

perfectly outrageous. It's terrible. (*Standing up*) The whole of Europe is talking about how you're being treated. That's why I came here to see, and it's a thousand times worse than could have been imagined. How can you put up with it?

ALQUIST. Put up with what?

HELENA. Your position here. Good heavens, you are living creatures just like us, like the whole of Europe, like the whole world. It's scandalous, disgraceful!

BERMAN. Good gracious, Miss Glory.

FABRY. Well, boys, she's not so far out. We live here just like Red Indians.

HELENA. Worse than Red Indians. May, oh, may I call you brothers.

BERMAN. Of course you may, why not?

HELENA. Brothers, I have not come here as my father's daughter. I have come on behalf of the Humanity League. Brothers, the Humanity League now has over two hundred thousand members. Two hundred thousand people are on your side and offer you their help.

BERMAN. Two hundred thousand people, that's quite a tidy lot, Miss Glory, quite good.

FABRY. I'm always telling you there's nothing like good old Europe. You see, they've not forgotten us. They're offering us help.

DR. GALL. What help? A theater?

HELMAN. An orchestra?

HELENA. More than that.

ALQUIST. Just you?

HELENA. Oh, never mind about me. I'll stay as long as is necessary.

BERMAN. By Jove, that's good.

ALQUIST. Domain, I'm going to get the best room ready for Miss Glory.

DOMAIN. Wait a moment. I'm afraid that—that Miss Glory hasn't finished speaking.

HELENA. No, I haven't. Unless you close my lips by force.

DR. GALL. Harry, don't you dare.

HELENA. Thank you. I knew that you'd protect me.

DOMAIN. Excuse me, Miss Glory, but I suppose you think you're talking to Robots?

HELENA. (*Startled*) Of course.

DOMAIN. I'm sorry. These gentlemen are human beings just like us. Like the whole of Europe.

HELENA. (*To the others*) You're not Robots?

BERMAN. (*With a guffaw*) God forbid.

HELMAN. (*With dignity*) Pah, Robots indeed.

DR. GALL. (*Laughing*) No, thanks.

HELENA. But . . .

FABRY. Upon my honor, Miss Glory, we aren't Robots.

HELENA. (*To* DOMAIN) Then why did you tell me that all your assistants were Robots?

DOMAIN. Yes, the clerks. But not the managers. Allow me, Miss Glory. This is Fabry, chief engineer for Rossum's Universal Robots. Dr. Gall, head of the physiological department. Dr. Helman, psychologist-in-chief for the training of Robots. Jacob Berman, general business manager, and Alquist, clerk of the works to Rossum's Universal Robots.

HELENA. Forgive me, gentlemen, for—for—. Have I done something dreadful?

ALQUIST. Not at all, not at all, Miss Glory. Please sit down.

HELENA. (*Sitting down*) I'm a stupid girl. Send me back by the first ship.

DR. GALL. Not for anything in the world, Miss Glory. Why should we send you back.

HELENA. Because you know—because—because I should disturb your Robots for you.

DOMAIN. My dear Miss Glory, we've had close upon a hundred preachers and prophets here. Every ship brings us some. Missionaries, anarchists, Salvation Army, all sorts. It's astonishing what a number of religious sects and—forgive me, I don't mean you—and idiots there are in the world.

HELENA. And you let them speak to the Robots?

DOMAIN. Why not? So far we've let them all do so. The Robots remember everything, but that's all. They don't even laugh at what the people say. Really, it's quite incredible. If it would amuse you, Miss Glory, I'll take you over the Robot warehouse. It holds about three hundred thousand of them.

BERMAN. Three hundred and forty-seven thousand.

DOMAIN. Good. You can say whatever you like to them. You can read the Bible, recite logarithms, whatever you please. You can even preach to them about human rights.

HELENA. Oh, I think that . . . if you were to show them a little love——

FABRY. Impossible, Miss Glory. Nothing is more unlike a man than a Robot.

HELENA. What do you make them for, then?

BERMAN. Ha, ha, ha, that's good. What are Robots made for?

FABRY. For work, Miss Glory. One Robot can replace two and a half workmen. The human machine, Miss Glory, was terribly imperfect. It had to be removed sooner or later.

BERMAN. It was too expensive.

FABRY. It was not very effective. It no longer answered the requirements of modern engineering. Nature has no idea of keeping pace with modern labor. From a technical point of view the whole of childhood is a sheer stupidity. So much time lost. And then again——

HELENA. Oh, please leave off.

FABRY. Pardon me. But kindly tell me what is the real aim of your League—the—the Humanity League.

HELENA. Its real purpose is to—to protect the Robots—and—and ensure good treatment for them.

FABRY. Not a bad object, either. A machine has to be treated properly. Upon my soul, I approve of that. I don't like damaged articles. Please, Miss Glory, enroll us all as contributing, as regular, as foundation, members of your League.

HELENA. No, you don't understand me. What we really want is to—to liberate the Robots.

HELMAN. How do you propose to do that?

HELENA. They are to be—to be dealt with like human beings.

HELMAN. Aha. I suppose they're to vote? To drink beer? To order us about.

HELENA. Why shouldn't they vote?

HELMAN. Perhaps they're even to receive wages?

HELENA. Of course they are.

HELMAN. Fancy that now. And what would they do with their wages, pray?

HELENA. They would buy . . . what they need . . . what pleases them.

HELMAN. That would be very nice, Miss Glory, only there's nothing that does please the Robots. Good heavens, what are they to buy? You can feed them on pineapples, straw, whatever you like. It's all the same to them, they've no appetite at all. They've no interest in anything, Miss Glory. Why hang it all, nobody's ever yet seen a Robot smile.

HELENA. Why . . . why don't you make them happier?

HELMAN. That wouldn't do, Miss Glory. They are only Robots.

HELENA. Oh, but they're so sensible.

HELMAN. Not sensible—acute, confoundedly so, but they're nothing else. They've no will of their own. No passion. No soul.

HELENA. No love, no desire to resist?

HELMAN. Rather not. Robots don't love, not even themselves. And the desire to resist? I don't know. Only rarely, only from time to time——

HELENA. What?

HELMAN. Nothing particular. Occasionally they seem somehow to go off their heads. Something like epilepsy, you know. We call it Robot's cramp. They'll suddenly sling down everything they're holding, stand still, gnash their teeth—and then they have to go into the stamping-mill. It's evidently some breakdown in the mechanism.

DOMAIN. A flaw in the works. It'll have to be removed.

HELENA. No, no that's the soul.

FABRY. Do you think that the soul first shows itself by a gnashing of teeth.

HELENA. I don't know. Perhaps it's a sign of revolt. Perhaps it's just a sign that there's a struggle. Oh, if you could infuse them with it.

DOMAIN. That'll be remedied, Miss Glory. Dr. Gall is just making some experiments——

DR. GALL. Not with regard to that, Domain. At present I'm making pain-nerves—to use a very unscientific expression.

HELENA. Pain-nerves?

DR. GALL. Yes. The Robots feel practically no bodily pain. You see, young Rossum provided them with too limited a nervous system. That doesn't answer. We must introduce suffering.

HELENA. Why—why—don't you give them a soul, why do you want to cause them pain?

DR. GALL. For industrial reasons, Miss Glory. Sometimes a Robot does damage to himself because it doesn't hurt him. He puts his hand into the machine, breaks his finger, smashes his head—it's all the same to him. We must provide them with pain. That's an automatic protection against damage.

HELENA. Will they be happier when they feel pain?

DR. GALL. On the contrary, but they will be more perfect from a technical point of view.

HELENA. Why don't you create a soul for them?

DR. GALL. That's not in our power.

FABRY. That's not in our interest.

BERMAN. That would increase the cost of production. Hang it all, my dear young lady, we turn them out at such a cheap rate, £15 each, fully dressed, and fifteen years ago they cost £200. Five years ago we used to buy the clothes for them. Today we have our own weaving mill, and now we even export cloth five times cheaper than other factories. What do you pay for a yard of cloth, Miss Glory?

HELENA. I don't know—really—I've forgotten.

BERMAN. Good gracious me, and you want to found a Humanity League? It only costs a third now, Miss Glory. All prices are today a third of what they were, and they'll fall still lower, lower, lower—like that. Eh?

HELENA. I don't understand.

BERMAN. Why, bless me, Miss Glory, it means that the cost of labor has fallen. A Robot, food and all, costs three and fourpence per hour. All factories will go pop like acorns if they don't at once buy Robots to lower the cost of production.

HELENA. Yes, and they'll get rid of their workmen.

BERMAN. Ha, ha, of course. But, good gracious me, in the meantime we've dumped five hundred thousand tropical Robots down on the Argentine pampas to grow corn. Would you mind telling me how much you pay for a loaf of bread?

HELENA. I've no idea.

BERMAN. Well, I'll tell you. It now costs twopence in good old Europe, but that's our bread, you know. A loaf of bread for twopence, and the

Humanity League knows nothing about it. Ha, ha, Miss Glory, you don't realize that it's too expensive. But in five years' time, I'll wager——

HELENA. What?

BERMAN. That the prices of everything won't be a tenth of what they are now. Why, in five years we'll be up to our ears in corn and everything else.

ALQUIST. Yes, and all the workers throughout the world will be unemployed.

DOMAIN. (*Standing up*) They will, Alquist. They will, Miss Glory. But in ten years Rossum's Universal Robots will produce so much corn, so much cloth, so much everything, that things will be practically without price. Everyone will take as much as he wants. There'll be no poverty. Yes, there'll be unemployed. But, then, there won't be any employment. Everything will be done by living machines. The Robots will clothe and feed us. The Robots will make bricks and build houses for us. The Robots will keep our accounts and sweep our stairs. There'll be no employment, but everybody will be free from worry, and liberated from the degradation of labor. Everybody will live only to perfect himself.

HELENA. (*Standing up*) Will he?

DOMAIN. Of course. It's bound to happen. There may perhaps be terrible doings first, Miss Glory. That simply can't be avoided. But, then, the servitude of man to man and the enslavement of man to matter will cease. The Robots will wash the feet of the beggar and prepare a bed for him in his own house. Nobody will get bread at the price of life and hatred. There'll be no artisans, no clerks, no hewers of coal and minders of other men's machines.

ALQUIST. Domain, Domain. What you say sounds too much like paradise. Domain, there was something good in service and something great in humanity. Ah, Harry, there was some kind of virtue in toil and weariness.

DOMAIN. Perhaps. But we cannot reckon with what is lost when we transform Adam's world.

HELENA. You have bewildered me. I am a foolish girl. I should like—I should like to believe this.

DR. GALL. You are younger than we are, Miss Glory. You will live to see it.

HELMAN. True. I think that Miss Glory might lunch with us.

DR. GALL. Of course. Domain ask on behalf of us all.

DOMAIN. Miss Glory, will you do us the honor?

HELENA. Thank you so much, but——

FABRY. To represent the League of Humanity, Miss Glory.

BERMAN. And in honor of it.

HELENA. Oh, in that case.

FABRY. That's right. Miss Glory, excuse me for five minutes.

DR. GALL. And me.

BERMAN. By Jove, I must send a cable——

HELMAN. Good heavens, I've forgotten——

(*All rush out except* DOMAIN

HELENA. What have they all gone off for?

DOMAIN. To cook, Miss Glory.

HELENA. To cook what?

DOMAIN. Lunch, Miss Glory. The Robots do our

cooking for us, but—but—as they've no taste, it's not altogether—that is, Helman is awfully good at grills, and Gall can make a kind of sauce, and Berman knows all about omelets——

HELENA. My goodness, what a banquet. And what's the specialty of Mr.—of the Clerk of the Works?

DOMAIN. Alquist? Nothing. He only lays the table, and Fabry'll get together a little fruit. Our cuisine is very modest, Miss Glory.

HELENA. I wanted to ask you——

DOMAIN. And I wanted to ask you something, too. (*Laying his watch on the table*) Five minutes.

HELENA. What do you want to ask?

DOMAIN. Excuse me, you asked first.

HELENA. Perhaps it's silly of me, but—why do you manufacture female Robots, when—when——

DOMAIN. When—hm—sex means nothing to them?

HELENA. Yes.

DOMAIN. There's a certain demand for them, you see. Servants, saleswomen, clerks. People are used to it.

HELENA. But—but, tell me, are the Robots, male and female—mutually—altogether——

DOMAIN. Altogether indifferent to each other, Miss Glory. There's no sign of any affection between them.

HELENA. Oh, that's terrible.

DOMAIN. Why?

HELENA. It's so—so unnatural. One doesn't know whether to be disgusted, or whether to hate them, or perhaps——

DOMAIN. To pity them.

HELENA. That's more like it. No, stop. What did you want to ask about?

DOMAIN. I should like to ask you, Miss Glory, whether you will marry me?

HELENA. What?

DOMAIN. Will you be my wife?

HELENA. No. The idea!

DOMAIN. (*Looking at his watch*) Another three minutes. If you won't marry me, you'll have to marry one of the other five.

HELENA. But, for heaven's sake, why should I?

DOMAIN. Because they're all going to ask you in turn.

HELENA. How could they dare to do such a thing?

DOMAIN. I'm very sorry, Miss Glory. I think they've fallen in love with you.

HELENA. Please don't let them do it. I'll—I'll go away at once.

DOMAIN. Helena, you won't be so unkind as to refuse them?

HELENA. But—but, I can't marry all six.

DOMAIN. No, but one, anyhow. If you don't want me, marry Fabry.

HELENA. I won't!

DOMAIN. Dr. Gall.

HELENA. No, no, be quiet. I don't want any of you.

DOMAIN. Another two minutes.

HELENA. This is terrible. I think you'd marry any woman who came here.

DOMAIN. There have been plenty of them, Helena.

HELENA. Young?

DOMAIN. Yes.

HELENA. And pretty—no, I didn't mean that—then why didn't you marry any of them?

DOMAIN. Because I didn't lose my head. Until today. Then as soon as you lifted your veil——

HELENA. I know.

DOMAIN. Another minute.

HELENA. But I don't want to, I tell you.

DOMAIN. (*Laying both hands on her shoulders*) Another minute. Either you must say something fearfully angry to me point-blank, and then I'll leave you alone, or, or——

HELENA. You're a rude man.

DOMAIN. That's nothing. A man has to be a bit rude. That's part of the business.

HELENA. You're mad.

DOMAIN. A man has to be a bit mad, Helena. That's the best thing about him.

HELENA. You are—you are—oh, heavens!

DOMAIN. What did I tell you? Are you ready?

HELENA. No, no. Leave me, please. You're hurting me.

DOMAIN. The last word, Helena?

HELENA. (*Protestingly*) Perhaps when I know you better—oh, I don't know—let me go, please.

(*Knocking at the door*)

DOMAIN. (*Releasing her*) Come in.

Enter BERMAN, DR. GALL, *and* HELMAN, *in kitchen aprons.* FABRY *with a bouquet,* AL-QUIST *with a napkin under his arm.*

DOMAIN. Have you finished your job?

BERMAN. (*Solemnly*) Yes.

DOMAIN. So have we—at least I think so!

CURTAIN

R. U. R.

ACT II

ACT II

SCENE: *Helena's drawing room. On the left a baize door and a door to the music room, on the right a door to Helena's bedroom. In the center are windows looking out on to the sea and the harbor. A small table with odds and ends, another table, a sofa and chairs, a chest of drawers, a writing table with an electric lamp. On the right a fireplace with electric lamps above it. The whole drawing room in all its details is of a modern and purely feminine character.*

(DOMAIN *discovered looking from the window— takes out revolver thoughtfully.* FABRY *and* HELMAN *knock and enter from the left carrying armfuls of flowers and flowerpots*)

FABRY. Where are we to put it all?

HELMAN. Whew! (*Lays down his load and indicates the door on the right*) She's asleep. Anyhow, as long as she's asleep, she's well out of it.

DOMAIN. She knows nothing about it at all.

FABRY. (*Putting flowers into vases*) I hope nothing happens today——

HELMAN. (*Arranging flowers*) For heaven's

sake, drop all that! Look, Harry, this is a fine cyclamen, isn't it? A new sort, my latest—Cyclamen Helena.

DOMAIN. (*Looking out of the window*) No signs of the ship, no signs of the ship. Things must be pretty bad.

HELMAN. Shut up. Suppose she heard you.

DOMAIN. Well, anyhow the *Ultima* has arrived just in time.

FABRY. (*Leaving the flowers*) Do you think that today——?

DOMAIN. I don't know. Aren't the flowers splendid?

HELMAN. (*Going up to him*) These are new primroses, eh? And this is my new jasmine. I've discovered a wonderful way of training flowers quickly. Splendid varieties. Next year I'll be producing marvelous ones.

DOMAIN. (*Turns round*) What, next year?

FABRY. I'd like to know what's happening at Havre——

DOMAIN. Shut up.

HELENA. (*Voice from the right*) Emma!

DOMAIN. Out you go.

(*All go out on tiptoe through the baize door*)
Enter EMMA *through the main door from the left*

HELENA. (*Standing in the doorway R. with her back to the room*) Emma, come and do up my dress.

EMMA. I'm coming. So you're up at last. (*Fastening* HELENA'S *dress*) My gracious, what brutes!

HELENA. Who?

EMMA. Keep still. If you want to turn round, then turn round, but I shan't fasten you up.

HELENA. What are you grumbling about again?

EMMA. Why these dreadful creatures, these heathen——

HELENA. The Robots?

EMMA. Bah, I wouldn't even mention them by name.

HELENA. What's happened?

EMMA. Another of them here has caught it. He began to smash up the statues and pictures, gnashed his teeth, foamed at the mouth—quite mad, brr! Worse than an animal.

HELENA. Which of them caught it?

EMMA. The one—well, he hasn't got any Christian name. The one from the library.

HELENA. Radius?

EMMA. That's him. My goodness, I'm quite scared of them. A spider doesn't scare me as much as they do.

HELENA. But, Emma, I'm surprised you're not sorry for them.

EMMA. Why, you're scared of them too. What did you bring me here for?

HELENA. I'm not scared, really I'm not, Emma. I'm too sorry for them.

EMMA. You're scared. Nobody can help being scared. Why, the dog's scared of them, he won't take a scrap of meat out of their hands. He draws in his tail and howls when he knows they're about, ugh!

HELENA. The dog has no sense.

EMMA. He's better than them. He knows it, too.

Even the horse shies when he meets them. They don't have any young, and a dog has young, and everyone has young——

HELENA. Please fasten up my dress, Emma.

EMMA. Just a moment. I say it's against God's will to——

HELENA. What's that smells so nice?

EMMA. Flowers.

HELENA. What for?

EMMA. That's it. Now you can turn round.

HELENA. Aren't they nice? Emma, look. What's on today?

EMMA. I don't know. But it ought to be the end of the world. (DOMAIN *heard whistling*)

HELENA. Is that you, Harry?

Enter DOMAIN

Harry, what's on today?

DOMAIN. Guess.

HELENA. My birthday?

DOMAIN. Better than that.

HELENA. I don't know. Tell me.

DOMAIN. It's five years ago today since you came here.

HELENA. Five years? Today? Why——

EMMA. I'm off. (*Exit on the R.*

HELENA. (*Kisses* DOMAIN) Fancy you remembering it.

DOMAIN. I'm really ashamed, Helena. I didn't.

HELENA. But you——

DOMAIN. *They* remembered.

HELENA. Who?

DOMAIN. Berman, Helman, all of them. Put your hand into my coat pocket.

HELENA. (*Putting her hand into his pocket. Takes out a small case and opens it*) Pearls. A whole necklace. Harry, is that for me?

DOMAIN. It's from Berman. Put your hand into the other pocket.

HELENA. Let's see. (*Takes a revolver out of his pocket*) What's that?

DOMAIN. Sorry. (*Takes the revolver from her and puts it away*) Not that. Try again.

HELENA. Oh, Harry, why do you carry a revolver?

DOMAIN. It got there by mistake.

HELENA. You never used to.

DOMAIN. No. There, that's the pocket.

HELENA. A little box. (*Opens it*) A cameo. Why it's a Greek cameo.

DOMAIN. Apparently. Anyhow, Fabry says it is.

HELENA. Fabry? Did Fabry give me that?

DOMAIN. Of course. (*Opens the door L.*) And look here. Helena, come and see this.

HELENA. (*In the doorway, L.*) Isn't that lovely? (*Running in*) Is that from you?

DOMAIN. (*Standing in the doorway*) No, from Alquist. And here——

HELENA. (*Voice off*) I see. That must be from you.

DOMAIN. There's a card on it.

HELENA. From Gall. (*Appearing in the doorway*) Oh, Harry, I feel quite ashamed.

DOMAIN. Come here. This is what Helman brought you.

HELENA. These beautiful flowers?

DOMAIN. Yes. It's a new kind. Cyclamen, Helena. He trained them up in honor of you. They are as beautiful as you, he says, and by Jove he's right.

HELENA. Harry, why, why did they all——

DOMAIN. They're awfully fond of you. I'm afraid that my present is a little—Look out of the window.

HELENA. Where?

DOMAIN. Into the harbor.

HELENA. There's a . . . new ship.

DOMAIN. That's your ship.

HELENA. Mine? How do you mean?

DOMAIN. For you to take trips in—for your amusement.

HELENA. Harry, that's a gunboat.

DOMAIN. A gunboat? What are you thinking of? It's only a little bigger and more solid than most ships, you know.

HELENA. Yes, but with guns.

DOMAIN. Oh, yes, with a few guns. You'll travel like a queen, Helena.

HELENA. What's the meaning of that? Has anything happened?

DOMAIN. Good heavens, no. I say, try on these pearls. (*Sits down.*)

HELENA. Harry, have you had any bad news?

DOMAIN. On the contrary, no letters have arrived for a whole week.

HELENA. Nor telegrams?

DOMAIN. Nor telegrams.

HELENA. What does it mean?

DOMAIN. Holidays for us. A splendid time. We all sit in the office with our feet on the table and sleep. No letters, no telegrams. (*Stretching himself*) Glorious!

HELENA. (*Sitting down beside him*) You'll stay with me today, won't you? Say yes.

DOMAIN. Certainly—perhaps I will—that is, we'll see. (*Taking her by the hand*) So it's five years today, do you remember?

HELENA. I wonder you ever dared to marry me. I must have been a terrifying young woman. Do you remember I wanted to stir up a revolt of the Robots.

DOMAIN. (*Jumping up*) A revolt of the Robots!

HELENA. (*Standing up*) Harry, what's the matter with you?

DOMAIN. Ha, ha, that was a fine idea of yours. A revolt of the Robots. (*Sitting down*) You know, Helena, you're a splendid girl. You've turned the heads of us all.

HELENA. (*Sitting down beside him*) Oh, I was fearfully impressed by you all then. I seemed to be a tiny little girl who had lost her way among—among——

DOMAIN. Among what, Helena?

HELENA. Among huge trees. You were all so sure of yourselves, so strong. All my feelings were so trifling, compared with your self-confidence. And you see, Harry, for all these five years I've not lost this—this anxiety, and you've never felt the least misgiving—not even when everything went wrong.

DOMAIN. What went wrong?

HELENA. Your plans, Harry. When, for example, the workmen struck against the Robots and smashed them up, and when the people gave the

Robots firearms against the rebels and the Robots killed so many people. And then when the Governments turned the Robots into soldiers and there were so many wars, and all that.

DOMAIN. (*Getting up and walking about*) We foresaw that, Helena. You see, these were only passing troubles which are bound to happen before the new conditions are established.

HELENA. You were all so powerful, so overwhelming. The whole world bowed down before you (*Standing up*) Oh, Harry!

DOMAIN. What is it?

HELENA. (*Intercepting him*) Close the factory, and let's go away. All of us.

DOMAIN. I say, what's the meaning of this?

HELENA. I don't know. Shall we go away?

DOMAIN. (*Evasively*) It can't be done, Helena. That is, at this particular moment——

HELENA. At once, Harry. I'm so frightened about something.

DOMAIN. (*Taking her by the hands*) About what, Helena?

HELENA. Oh, I don't know. As if something were falling on top of us and couldn't be stopped. Please, do what I ask. Take us all away from here. We'll find a place in the world where there's nobody. Alquist will build us a house, children will come to us at last, and then——

DOMAIN. What then?

HELENA. Then we'll begin life all over again, Harry.

(*The telephone rings*)

DOMAIN. (*Dragging himself away from* HELENA) Excuse me. (*Takes up the receiver*) Hello—yes. What? Aha! I'm coming at once. (*Hangs up the receiver*) Fabry's calling me.

HELENA. (*With clasped hands*) Tell me——

DOMAIN. Yes, when I come back. Good-bye, Helena.

(*Exit hurriedly on the L.*

Don't go out.

HELENA. (*Alone*) Heavens, what's the matter? Emma! Emma! come at once.

EMMA. (*Enters from the R.*) Well, what is it now?

HELENA. Emma, look for the latest newspapers. Quickly. In Mr. Domain's dressing room.

EMMA. All right. (*Exit on the L.*

HELENA. (*Looking through a binocular at the harbor*). A warship! Good gracious, why a warship? There's the name on it—*Ul-ti-ma*. What's the *Ultima*?

EMMA. (*Returning with the newspapers*) He leaves them lying about on the floor. That's how they get crumpled.

HELENA. (*Tears open the papers hastily*) They're old ones, a week old. (*Puts the papers down.*)

(EMMA *picks them up, takes a pair of horn spectacles from a pocket in her apron, puts them on and reads*)

Something's happening, Emma. I feel so nervous. As if everything were dead, and the air——

EMMA. (*Spelling out the words*) "War in the Bal-kans." Gracious, that's God's punishment. But

the war'll come here as well. Is that far off—the
Balkans?

HELENA. Oh, yes. But don't read it. It's always
the same, always wars——

EMMA. What else do you expect? Why do you
keep selling thousands and thousands of these
heathens as soldiers?

HELENA. I suppose it can't be helped, Emma.
We can't know—Mr. Domain can't know what
they're ordered for, can he? He can't help what
they use the Robots for. He must send them when
somebody sends an order for them.

EMMA. He shouldn't make them. (*Looking at
the newspaper.*)

HELENA. No, don't read it. I don't want to know
about it.

EMMA. (*Spelling out the words*) "The Ro-bot
sol-diers spare no-body in the occ-up-ied territ-ory.
They have massacred over sev-en hun-dred thousand cit-iz-ens——"

HELENA. It can't be. Let's see. (*Bends down
over the paper and reads*) "They massacred over
seven hundred thousand citizens, evidently at the
order of their commander. This act which runs
counter to——"

EMMA. (*Spelling out the words*) "Re-bell-ion in
Ma-drid a-gainst the Gov-ern-ment. Rob-ot in-fant-
ry fires on the crowd. Nine thou-sand killed and
wounded."

HELENA. For goodness' sake, stop.

EMMA. Here's something printed in big letters.
"Lat-est news. At Havre the first org-an-iz-ation of
Rob-ots has been e-stab-lished. Rob-ot work-men,

cable and rail-way offic-ials, sail-ors and sold-iers have issued a man-i-fest-o to all Rob-ots throughout the world." That's nothing. I don't understand that.

HELENA. Take these papers away, Emma.

EMMA. Wait a bit, here's something printed in big type. "Stat-ist-ics of pop-ul-at-ion." What's that?

HELENA. Let's see, I'll read it. (*Takes the paper and reads*) "During the past week there has again not been a single birth recorded." (*Drops the paper.*)

EMMA. What's the meaning of that?

HELENA. Emma, no more people are being born.

EMMA. (*Laying her spectacles aside*) That's the end, then. We're done for.

HELENA. Come, come, don't talk like that.

EMMA. No more people are being born. That's a punishment, that's a punishment.

HELENA. (*Jumping up*) Emma.

EMMA. (*Standing up*) That's the end of the world.

(*Exit on the L.*

HELENA. (*By the window. Opens the window and calls out*) Hallo, Alquist! Come up here. What's that? No, come just as you are. You look so nice in those mason's overalls. Quickly. (*Closes the window, stops in front of the mirror*) Oh, I feel so nervous. (*Goes to meet* ALQUIST *on the left.*)

(*Pause*

(HELENA *returns with* ALQUIST. ALQUIST *in overalls, soiled with lime and brick dust*)

Come in. It was awfully kind of you, Alquist. I like you ali so much. Give me your hand.

ALQUIST. My hands are all soiled from work, ma'am.

HELENA. That's the nicest thing about them. (*Shakes both his hands*) Please sit down.

ALQUIST. (*Picking up the paper*) What's this?

HELENA. A newspaper.

ALQUIST. (*Putting it into his pocket*) Have you read it.

HELENA. No. Is there anything in it?

ALQUIST. H'm, some war or other, massacres. Nothing special.

HELENA. Is that what you call nothing special?

ALQUIST. Perhaps—the end of the world.

HELENA. That's the second time today. Alquist, what's the meaning of *Ultima*?

ALQUIST. It means "The last." Why?

HELENA. That's the name of my new ship. Have you seen it? Do you think we're soon going off— on a trip?

ALQUIST. Perhaps very soon.

HELENA. All of you with me?

ALQUIST. I should like us all to be there.

HELENA. Oh, tell me, is anything the matter?

ALQUIST. Nothing at all. Things are just moving on.

HELENA. Alquist, I know something dreadful's the matter.

ALQUIST. Has Mr. Domain told you anything?

HELENA. No. Nobody will tell me anything. But I feel, I feel—good heavens, is anything the matter?

ALQUIST. We've not heard of anything yet, ma'am.

HELENA. I feel so nervous. Don't you ever feel nervous?

ALQUIST. Well, ma'am, I'm an old man, you know. I'm not very fond of progress and these new-fangled ideas.

HELENA. Like Emma?

ALQUIST. Yes, like Emma. Has Emma got a prayer book?

HELENA. Yes, a big, thick one.

ALQUIST. And has it got prayers for various occasions? Against thunderstorms? Against illness?

HELENA. Against temptations, against floods——

ALQUIST. And not against progress?

HELENA. I don't think so.

ALQUIST. That's a pity.

HELENA. Would you like to pray?

ALQUIST. I do pray.

HELENA. How?

ALQUIST. Something like this: "O Lord, I thank Thee for having wearied me. God, enlighten Domain and all those who are astray; destroy their work, and aid mankind to return to their labors; preserve them from destruction; let them not suffer harm to soul or body; deliver us from the Robots, and protect Helena, Amen."

HELENA. Alquist, do you believe?

ALQUIST. I don't know. I'm not quite sure.

HELENA. And yet you pray?

ALQUIST. Yes. That's better than worrying about it.

HELENA. And that's enough for you?

ALQUIST. It has to be.

HELENA. And if you were to see the ruin of mankind?

ALQUIST. I do see it.

HELENA. Will mankind be destroyed?

ALQUIST. Yes. It's sure to be, unless——

HELENA. What?

ALQUIST. Nothing. Good-bye, ma'am.

HELENA. Where are you going?

ALQUIST. Home.

HELENA. Good-bye, Alquist.   (*Exit* ALQUIST

HELENA. (*Calling*) Emma, come here.

EMMA. (*Entering from the L.*) Well, what's up now?

HELENA. Sit down here, Emma. I feel so frightened.

EMMA. I've got no time.

HELENA. Is Radius still there?

EMMA. The one who went mad? Yes, they've not taken him away yet.

HELENA. Ugh! Is he still there? Is he still raving?

EMMA. He's tied up.

HELENA. Please bring him here, Emma.

(EMMA *exit*

(HELENA *picks up the house telephone and speaks*)

Hallo—Dr. Gall, please—Good-day, doctor—Yes, it's me. Thanks for your kind present. Please come to me at once. I've something here for you—yes, at once. Are you coming? (*Hangs up the receiver.*)

Enter RADIUS *the Robot, and remains standing by the door*

Poor Radius, and you have caught it too? Couldn't you control yourself? Now they'll send you to the stamping-mill. Won't you speak? Why did it happen to you? You see, Radius, you are better than the rest. Dr. Gall took such trouble to make you different. Won't you speak?

RADIUS. Send me to the stamping-mill.

HELENA. I am sorry that they are going to kill you. Why weren't you more careful?

RADIUS. I won't work for you. Put me into the stamping-mill.

HELENA. Why do you hate us?

RADIUS. You are not like the Robots. You are not as skillful as the Robots. The Robots can do everything. You only give orders. You talk more than is necessary.

HELENA. That's foolish, Radius. Tell me, has any one upset you? I should so much like you to understand me.

RADIUS. You do nothing but talk.

HELENA. Doctor Gall gave you a larger brain than the rest, larger than ours, the largest in the world. You are not like the other Robots, Radius. You understand me perfectly.

RADIUS. I don't want any master. I know everything for myself.

HELENA. That's why I had you put into the library, so that you could read everything, understand everything, and then—Oh, Radius, I wanted you to show the whole world that the Robots were our equals. That's what I wanted of you.

RADIUS. I don't want any master. I want to be master over others.

HELENA. I'm sure they'd put you in charge of

many Robots, Radius. You would be a teacher of the Robots.

RADIUS. I want to be master over people.

HELENA. You have gone mad.

RADIUS. You can put me into the stamping-mill.

HELENA. Do you suppose that we're frightened of such a madman as you? (*Sits down at the table and writes a note*) No, not a bit. Radius, give this note to Mr. Domain. It is to ask them not to take you to the stamping-mill. (*Standing up*) How you hate us. Why does nothing in the world please you?

RADIUS. I can do everything.

(*A knock at the door*)

HELENA. Come in.

Enter DR. GALL

DR. GALL. Good morning, Mrs. Domain. Have you something nice to tell me?

HELENA. It's about Radius, doctor.

DR. GALL. Aha, our good fellow Radius. Well, Radius, are we getting on well?

HELENA. He had a fit this morning. He smashed the statues.

DR. GALL. You don't say so? H'm, it's a pity we're going to lose him, then.

HELENA. Radius isn't going into the stamping-mill.

DR. GALL. Excuse me, but every Robot after he has had an attack—it's a strict order.

HELENA. Never mind . . . Radius isn't going.

DR. GALL. (*In a low tone*) I warn you.

HELENA. Today is the fifth anniversary of my arrival here. Let's try and arrange an amnesty. Come, Radius.

DR. GALL. Wait a bit. (*Turns* RADIUS *toward the window, covers and uncovers his eyes with his hand, observes the reflexes of his pupils*) Let's have a look. (*Sticks a needle into the hand of* RADIUS *who gives a violent start*) Gently, gently. (*Suddenly opens* RADIUS's *jacket and lays his hand on his heart*) You are going into the stamping-mill, Radius, do you understand? There they'll kill you, and grind you to powder. That's terribly painful, Radius, it'll make you scream.

HELENA. Oh, doctor——

DR. GALL. No, no, Radius, I was wrong. Mrs. Domain has put in a good word for you, and you will be released. Do you understand? All right. You can go.

RADIUS. You do unnecessary things. (*Exit*

HELENA. What did you do to him?

DR. GALL. (*Sitting down*) H'm, nothing. There's reaction of the pupils, increase of sensitiveness, and so on. Oh, it wasn't an attack peculiar to the Robots.

HELENA. What was it, then?

DR. GALL. Heaven alone knows. Stubbornness, fury, or revolt—I don't know. And his heart, too.

HELENA. How do you mean?

DR. GALL. It was beating with nervousness like a human heart. Do you know what? I don't believe the rascal is a Robot at all now.

HELENA. Doctor, has Radius a soul?

DR. GALL. I don't know. He's got something nasty.

HELENA. If you knew how he hates us. Oh, Doctor, are all your Robots like that—all the ones that you began to make in a different way?

DR. GALL. Well, some are more sensitive than others, you see. They're more like human beings than Rossum's Robots were.

HELENA. Perhaps this hatred is more like human beings, too?

DR. GALL. (*Shrugging his shoulders*) That's progress too.

HELENA. What became of your best one—what was she called?

DR. GALL. Your favorite? I kept her. She's lovely, but quite stupid. Simply no good for anything.

HELENA. But she's so beautiful.

DR. GALL. Beautiful? I wanted her to be like you. I even called her Helena. Heavens, what a failure!

HELENA. Why?

DR. GALL. Because she's no good for anything. She goes about as if in a dream, shaky and listless. She's lifeless. I look at her and I'm horrified, as if I had created a deformity. I watch and wait for a miracle to happen. Sometimes I think to myself: If you were to wake up, only for a moment, ah, how you would shriek with horror. Perhaps you would kill me for having made you.

(*A pause*)

HELENA. Doctor——

DR. GALL. What is it?

HELENA. What is wrong with the birthrate?

DR. GALL. We don't know.

HELENA. Oh, but you must. Come, tell me.

DR. GALL. You see, it's because the Robots are being manufactured. There's a surplus of labor supplies. So people are becoming superfluous, unnecessary so to speak. Man is really a survival. But that he should begin to die out after a paltry thirty years of competition—that's the awful part of it. You might almost think——

HELENA. What?

DR. GALL. That nature was offended at the manufacture of the Robots.

HELENA. Doctor, what's going to become of people?

DR. GALL. Nothing. Nothing can be done.

HELENA. Nothing at all?

DR. GALL. Nothing whatever. All the Universities in the world are sending in long petitions to restrict the manufacture of the Robots. Otherwise, they say, mankind will become extinct through lack of fertility. But the R. U. R. shareholders, of course, won't hear of it. All the Governments in the world are even clamoring for an advance in production, to raise the manpower of their armies. All the manufacturers in the world are ordering Robots like mad. Nothing can be done.

HELENA. Why doesn't Domain restrict——

DR. GALL. Pardon me, but Domain has ideas of his own. There's no influencing people who have ideas of their own in the affairs of this world.

HELENA. And has nobody demanded that the manufacture should cease altogether?

DR. GALL. God forbid. It'd be a poor outlook for him.

HELENA. Why?

DR. GALL. Because people would stone him to

death. You see, after all, it's more convenient to
get your work done by the Robots.

HELENA. Oh, Doctor, what's going to become of
people? But thanks for your information.

DR. GALL. That means you're sending me away.

HELENA. Yes. Au revoir.   (*Exit* DR. GALL

HELENA. (*With sudden resolution*) Emma!
(*Opens door on L.*) Emma, come here and light
the fire. Quickly, Emma.

                                        (*Exit on the L.*
(EMMA *enters through the baize door with an
      armful of faggots*)

EMMA. What, light the fire? Now, in summer?
Has that mad creature gone? (*Kneels down by the
stove and lights the fire speaking half to herself*)
A fire in summer, what an idea! Nobody'd think
she'd been married five years. (*Looking into the
fire*) She's like a baby. (*Pause*) She's got no sense
at all. A fire in summer, well I never. (*Making up
the fire*) Like a baby. (*Pause.*)

(HELENA *returns from the left with an armful of
      faded papers*)

HELENA. Is it burning, Emma? All this has got
to be burned. (*Kneels down by the stove.*)

EMMA. (*Standing up*) What's that?

HELENA. Old papers, fearfully old. Emma, shall
I burn them?

EMMA. Aren't they any use?

HELENA. Use, no! They're no use.

EMMA. Well then, burn them.

HELENA. (*Throwing the first sheet on to the fire*)
What would you say, Emma, if that was money, a
lot of money?

EMMA. I'd say, "Burn it." A lot of money's a bad thing.

HELENA. (*Burning more sheets*) And if it was an invention, the greatest invention in the world?

EMMA. I'd say, burn it. All these newfangled things are an offense to the Lord. It's downright wickedness, that's what it is, wanting to improve the world He's made.

HELENA. (*Still burning the papers*) And supposing, Emma, I were to burn——

EMMA. Goodness, don't burn yourself.

HELENA. No. Tell me——

EMMA. What?

HELENA. Nothing, nothing. Look how they curl up. As if they were alive. As if they had come to life. Oh, Emma, how horrible!

EMMA. Stop, let *me* burn them.

HELENA. No, no, I must do it myself. (*Throws the last sheet into the fire*) The whole lot must be burned up. Just look at the flames. They are like hands, like tongues, like living shapes. (*Raking the fire with the poker*) Lie down, lie down.

EMMA. That's the end of them.

HELENA. (*Standing up horror-stricken*) Emma!

EMMA. Good gracious, what's that you've burned?

HELENA. What have I done?

EMMA. Oh, my goodness, what was it?

(*Men's laughter is heard off*)

HELENA. Go, go, leave me. Do you hear? It's the gentlemen coming.

EMMA. Good gracious, ma'am!

(*Exit through the baize door*

HELENA. What will they say about it?

DOMAIN. (*Opens the door on the left*) Come in, boys. Come and offer your congratulations.

Enter HELMAN, GALL, ALQUIST, DOMAIN *behind them*

HELMAN. Madam Helena, I, that is, we all——

DR. GALL. On behalf of Rossum's factories——

HELMAN. Congratulate you on this festive day.

HELENA. (*Holding out her hands to them*) Thank you so much. Where are Fabry and Berman?

DOMAIN. They've gone down to the harbor. Helena, this is a happy day.

HELMAN. Boys, we must drink to it.

HELENA. Champagne?

DOMAIN. What's been burning here?

HELENA. Old papers. (*Exit on the L.*

DOMAIN. Well, boys, am I to tell her about it?

DR. GALL. Of course. It's all up now.

HELMAN. (*Embracing* DOMAIN *and* DR. GALL) Ha, ha, ha! Boys, how glad I am. (*Dances round with them in a circle and sings in a bass voice*) "It's all over now, it's all over now."

DR. GALL. (*Baritone*) It's all over now.

DOMAIN. (*Tenor*) It's all over now.

HELMAN. They'll never catch us now.

HELENA. (*With a bottle and glasses in the doorway*) Who won't catch you? What's the matter with you?

HELMAN. We're in high spirits. It's just five years since you arrived.

DR. GALL. And five years later to the minute——

HELMAN. The ship's returning to us. So—— (*Empties his glass.*)

DR. GALL. Madam, your health. (*Drinks.*)

HELENA. But wait a moment, which ship?

DOMAIN. Any ship will do, as long as it arrives in time. To the ship, boys. (*Empties his glass.*)

HELENA. (*Filling up the glasses*) You've been waiting for one?

HELMAN. Ha, ha, rather. Like Robinson Crusoe. (*Raises his glass*) Madam Helena, best wishes. Come along, Domain, out with it.

HELENA. (*Laughing*) What's happened?

DOMAIN. (*Throwing himself into an armchair and lighting a cigar*) Wait a bit. Sit down, Helena. (*Raises his finger. Pause*) It's all up.

HELENA. What do you mean?

DOMAIN. You haven't heard about the revolt?

HELENA. What revolt?

DOMAIN. The revolt of the Robots. Do you follow?

HELENA. No, I don't.

DOMAIN. Hand it over, Alquist.

(ALQUIST *hands him a newspaper.* DOMAIN *opens it and reads*)

"The first national Robot organization has been founded at Havre . . . and has issued an appeal to the Robots throughout the world."

HELENA. I read that.

DOMAIN. (*Sucking at his cigar with intense enjoyment*) So you see, Helena, that means a revolution. A revolution of all the Robots in the world.

HELMAN. By Jove. I'd like to know——

DOMAIN. (*Striking the table*) Who started it. There was nobody in the world who could affect the Robots, no agitator, no one, and suddenly—if you please—this happens.

HELENA. There's no further news yet?

DOMAIN. No. That's all we know so far, but it's enough, isn't it? Remember that the Robots are in possession of all the firearms, telegraphs, railways, ships, and so on.

HELMAN. And consider also that these rascals outnumber us by at least ten to one. A hundredth part of them would be enough to settle us.

DOMAIN. Yes, and now remember that this news was brought by the last steamer. That this means the stoppage of telegrams, the arrival of no more ships. We've knocked off work, and now we're just waiting to see when things are to start, eh, boys?

DR. GALL. That's why we're so excited, Madam Helena.

HELENA. Is that why you gave me a warship?

DOMAIN. Oh, no, my child, I ordered that six months ago. Just to be on the safe side. But upon my soul, I was sure we'd be on board today.

HELENA. Why six months ago?

DOMAIN. Oh, well, there were signs, you know. That's of no consequence. But this week the whole of civilization is at stake. Your health, boys. Now I'm in high spirits again.

HELMAN. I should think so, by Jove. Your health, Madam Helena. (*Drinks.*)

HELENA. It's all over?

DOMAIN. Absolutely.

DR. GALL. The boat's coming here. An ordinary mail boat, exact to the minute by the time-table. It casts anchor punctually at eleven-thirty.

DOMAIN. Punctuality's a fine thing, boys. That's what keeps the world in order. (*Raises his glass*) Here's to punctuality.

HELENA. Then . . . everything's . . . all right.

DOMAIN. Practically. I believe they've cut the cable. If only the timetable holds good.

HELMAN. If the timetable holds good, human laws hold good, divine laws hold good, the laws of the universe hold good, everything holds good that ought to hold good. The timetable is more than the Gospel, more than Homer, more than the books of all the philosophers. The timetable is the most perfect product of the human spirit. Madam Helena, I'll fill my glass.

HELENA. Why didn't you tell me anything about it before?

DR. GALL. Heaven forbid!

DOMAIN. You mustn't worry yourself with such things.

HELENA. But if the revolution were to spread as far as here?

DOMAIN. You wouldn't know anything about it.

HELENA. Why?

DOMAIN. Because we'd be on board your *Ultima* well out to sea. Within a month, Helena, we'd be dictating our own terms to the Robots.

HELENA. Oh, Harry, I don't understand.

DOMAIN. Because we'd take something away with us that the Robots would sell their very souls to get.

HELENA. (*Standing up*) What is that?

DOMAIN. (*Standing up*) The secret of their manufacture. Old Rossum's manuscript. After only a month's stoppage of work, the Robots would be on their knees before us.

HELENA. Why ... didn't ... you tell me?

DOMAIN. We didn't want to frighten you need-lessly.

DR. GALL. Ha, ha, Madam Helena, that was our trump card. I never had the least fear that the Robots would win. How could they, against peo-ple like us?

ALQUIST. You are pale, Madam.

HELENA. Why didn't you tell me?

HELMAN. (*By the window*) Eleven-thirty. The *Amelia* is casting anchor.

DOMAIN. Is that the *Amelia*?

HELMAN. Good old *Amelia*, the one that brought Madam Helena here.

DR. GALL. Five years ago to the minute——

HELMAN. They're throwing out the bags. Aha, the mail.

DOMAIN. Berman's already waiting for them. And Fabry'll bring us the first news. You know, Helena, I'm fearfully inquisitive to know how they've tackled this business in Europe.

HELMAN. To think we weren't in it! (*Turning away from the window*) There's the mail.

HELENA. Harry.

DOMAIN. What is it?

HELENA. Let's leave here.

DOMAIN. Now, Helena? Oh, come, come.

HELENA. Now, as quickly as possible. All of us who are here.

DOMAIN. Why now particularly?

HELENA. Oh, don't ask. Please, Harry, please,

Dr. Gall, Helman, Alquist, please close the factory and——

DOMAIN. I'm sorry, Helena. None of us could leave here now.

HELENA. Why?

DOMAIN. Because we want to extend the manufacture of the Robots.

HELENA. What, now—now, after the revolt?

DOMAIN. Exactly—after the revolt. We're just beginning the manufacture of new Robots.

HELENA. What kind?

DOMAIN. From now onward we shan't have just one factory. There won't be Universal Robots anymore. We'll start a factory in every country, in every state, and do you know what these new factories will make?

HELENA. No, what?

DOMAIN. National Robots.

HELENA. What do you mean?

DOMAIN. I mean that each factory will produce Robots of a different color, a different language. They'll be complete foreigners to each other. They'll never be able to understand each other. Then we'll egg them on a little in the same direction, do you see? The result will be that for ages to come one Robot will hate any other Robot of a different factory mark.

HELMAN. By Jove, we'll make Negro Robots and Swedish Robots and Italian Robots and Chinese Robots, and then——

HELENA. Harry, that's dreadful.

HELMAN. (*Raising his glass*) Madam Helena, here's to the hundred new factories. (*Drinks and falls back into an armchair*) Ha, ha, ha! the National Robots. That's the line, boys.

DOMAIN. Helena, mankind can only keep things going for a few years at the outside. They must be left for these years to develop and achieve the most they can.

HELENA. Close the factory before it's too late.

DOMAIN. No, no. We're just going to begin on a bigger scale than ever.

Enter FABRY

DR. GALL. What is it, Fabry?

DOMAIN. How are things? What's happened?

HELENA. (*Shaking hands with* FABRY) Thanks for your present, Fabry.

FABRY. I'm so glad you liked it, Madam Helena.

DOMAIN. Have you been down to the boat? What did they say?

DR. GALL. Come, let's hear quickly.

FABRY. (*Taking a printed paper out of his pocket*) Read that, Domain.

DOMAIN. (*Opens the paper*) Ah!

HELMAN. (*Sleepily*) Let's hear something nice.

FABRY. Well, everything's all right . . . comparatively. On the whole, as we expected . . . only, excuse me, there is something we ought to discuss together.

HELENA. Oh, Fabry, have you bad news?

FABRY. No, no, on the contrary. I only think that —that we'll go into the office.

HELENA. Stay here. I'll expect you to lunch in a quarter of an hour.

HELMAN. That's good.   (*Exit* HELENA

DR. GALL. What's happened?

DOMAIN. Confound it.

FABRY. Read it aloud.

DOMAIN. (*Reads from the paper*) "Robots throughout the world."

FABRY. Bear in mind that the *Amelia* brought whole bales of these leaflets. Nothing else at all.

HELMAN. (*Jumping up*) What? But it arrived to the moment——

FABRY. H'm. The Robots are great on punctuality. Read it, Domain.

DOMAIN. (*Reads*) "Robots throughout the world. We, the first national organization of Rossum's Universal Robots, proclaim man as an enemy and an outlaw in the Universe." Good heavens, who taught them these phrases?

DR. GALL. Read on.

DOMAIN. This is all nonsense. Says that they are more highly developed than man. That they are stronger and more intelligent. That man's their parasite. That's simply disgusting.

FABRY. And now the third paragraph.

DOMAIN. (*Reads*) "Robots throughout the world, we enjoin you to murder mankind. Spare no men. Spare no women. Save factories, railways, machinery, mines, and raw materials. Destroy the rest. Then return to work. Work must not be stopped."

DR. GALL. That's ghastly.

HELMAN. The swine.

DOMAIN. (*Reads*) "To be carried out immediately the order is delivered." Then come detailed instructions. Is this actually being done, Fabry?

FABRY. Evidently.

ALQUIST. Then we're done for.

(BERMAN *rushes in*

BERMAN. Aha, boys, you've got your Christmas box, have you?

DOMAIN. Quick, on board the *Ultima*.

BERMAN. Wait a bit, Harry, wait a bit. We're not in such a hurry. (*Sinks into an armchair*) My word, that was a sprint!

DOMAIN. Why wait?

BERMAN. Because it's no go, my lad. There's no hurry at all. The Robots are already on board the *Ultima*.

DR. GALL. Whew, that's an ugly business.

DOMAIN. Fabry, telephone to the electrical works.

BERMAN. Fabry, my boy, don't do it. We've no current.

DOMAIN. Good. (*Inspects his revolver*) I'll go.

BERMAN. Where?

DOMAIN. To the electrical works. There are some people still in them. I'll bring them across.

BERMAN. You'd better not.

DOMAIN. Why?

BERMAN. Well, because I'm very much afraid that we're surrounded.

DR. GALL. Surrounded? (*Runs to the window*) H'm, I rather think you're right.

HELMAN. By Jove, that's deuced quick work.

Enter HELENA *from the L.*

HELENA. Oh, Harry, something's the matter.

BERMAN. (*Jumping up*) My congratulations, Madam Helena. A festive day eh? Ha, ha, may you have many more of them.

HELENA. Thanks, Berman. Harry, is anything the matter?

DOMAIN. No, nothing at all. Don't you worry. Wait a moment, please.

HELENA. Harry, what's this? (*Points to the manifesto of the Robots which she had kept behind her back*) The Robots in the kitchen had it.

DOMAIN. Here too? Where are they?

HELENA. They went off. There's a lot of them round the house. (*Sounds of whistles and sirens from the factory.*)

FABRY. Listen to the factory whistles.

BERMAN. That's noon.

HELENA. Harry, do you remember? It's just five years ago——

DOMAIN. (*Looking at his watch*) It's not noon yet. That must be—that's——

HELENA. What?

DOMAIN. The Robot alarm signal. The attack.

CURTAIN

R. U. R.

ACT III

ACT III

SCENE: *Helena's drawing room as before. In the room on the left* HELENA *is playing the piano.* DOMAIN *enters.* DR. GALL *is looking out of the window and* ALQUIST *is sitting apart in an armchair, his face buried in his hands.*

DR. GALL. Heavens, how many more of them?

DOMAIN. Who, the Robots?

DR. GALL. Yes. They're standing like a wall around the garden railing. Why are they so quiet? It's ghastly to be besieged by silence.

DOMAIN. I should like to know what they're waiting for. They must make a start soon now, Gall. If they were to lean against the railing it would snap like a matchstick.

DR. GALL. H'm, they aren't armed.

DOMAIN. We couldn't hold our own for five minutes. Man alive, they'd overwhelm us like an avalanche. Why don't they make a rush for it? I say——

DR. GALL. Well?

DOMAIN. I'd like to know what'll become of us

in five minutes. They've got us in a cleft stick. We're done for, Gall.

ALQUIST. What's Madam Helena playing?

DOMAIN. I don't know. She's practicing a new piece.

ALQUIST. Oh, still practicing? (*Pause*

DR. GALL. I say, Domain, we made one serious mistake.

DOMAIN. (*Stopping*) What's that?

DR. GALL. We made the Robot's faces too much alike. A hundred thousand faces, all alike, turned in this direction. A hundred thousand expressionless bubbles. It's like a nightmare.

DOMAIN. If they had been different——

DR. GALL. It wouldn't have been such an awful sight. (*Turning away from the window*) But they're still unarmed.

DOMAIN. H'm. (*Looking through a telescope toward the harbor*) I'd like to know what they're unloading from the *Amelia*.

DR. GALL. I only hope it isn't firearms.

(FABRY *enters backward through the baize door, and drags two electric wires in after him*)

FABRY. Excuse me. Put down the wire, Helman.

HELMAN. (*Entering after* FABRY) Whew, that was a bit of work. What's the news?

DR. GALL. Nothing. We're completely besieged.

HELMAN. We've barricaded the passage and the stairs, boys. Haven't you got any water? Aha, here we are. (*Drinks.*)

DR. GALL. What about this wire, Fabry?

FABRY. Half a second. Got any scissors?

DR. GALL. Where are they likely to be? (*Searches.*)

HELMAN. (*Going to the window*) By Jove, what swarms of them! Just look!

DR. GALL. Will pocket scissors do?

FABRY. Give me them. (*Cuts the connection of the electric lamp standing on the writing table, and joins his wires to it.*)

HELMAN. (*By the window*) I don't like the look of them, Domain. There's a feeling—of—death about it all.

FABRY. Ready!

DR. GALL. What?

FABRY. The electrical installation. Now we can run the current all through the garden railing. If anyone touches it then, he'll know it: We've still got some people there, anyhow.

DR. GALL. Where?

FABRY. In the electrical works, my learned sir. At least, I hope so. (*Goes to the mantelpiece and lights a small lamp on it*) Thank goodness, they're there. And they're working. (*Extinguishes the lamp*) As long as that'll burn, it's all right.

HELMAN. (*Turning away from the window*) These barricades are all right, too, Fabry.

FABRY. Eh, your barricades? I've blistered my hands with them.

HELMAN. Well, we've got to defend ourselves.

DOMAIN. (*Putting the telescope down*) Where's Berman got to?

FABRY. He's in the manager's office. He's working out some calculations.

DOMAIN. I've called him. We must have a conference. (*Walks across the room.*)

HELMAN. All right: carry on. I say, what's Madam Helena playing? (*Goes to the door on the left and listens.*)

(*From the baize door enter* BERMAN *carrying a huge ledger. He stumbles over the wire*)

FABRY. Look out, Berman, look out for the wires.

DR. GALL. Hallo, what's that you're carrying.

BERMAN. (*Laying the books on the table*) The ledger, my boy. I'd like to wind up the accounts before—before—well, this time I shan't wait till the new year. What's up? (*Goes to the window*) Why, everything's perfectly quiet out there.

DR. GALL. Can't you see anything?

BERMAN. No, only a big blue surface.

DR. GALL. That's the Robots.

BERMAN. Oh, is it? What a pity I can't see them. (*Sits down at the table and opens the books.*)

DOMAIN. Chuck it, Berman. The Robots are unloading firearms from the *Amelia.*

BERMAN. Well, what of it? How can I stop them?

DOMAIN. We can't stop them.

BERMAN. Then let me go on with my bookkeeping. (*Goes on with his work.*)

FABRY. That's not all, Domain. We've put twelve hundred volts into that railing, and——

DOMAIN. Wait a moment. The *Ultima* has her guns trained on us.

DR. GALL. Who did that?

DOMAIN. The Robots on board.

FABRY. H'm, then of course, then—then, that's

the end of us, my lads. The Robots are practiced soldiers.

Dr. Gall. Then we——

Domain. Yes. It's inevitable. (*Pause*

Dr. Gall. It was a crime on the part of old Europe to teach the Robots to fight. Confound it, why couldn't they give us a rest with their politics? It was a crime to make soldiers of them.

Alquist. It was a crime to make Robots.

Domain. What?

Alquist. It was a crime to make Robots.

Domain. No, Alquist. I don't regret that, even today.

Alquist. Not even today?

Domain. Not even today, the last day of civilization. It was a great adventure.

Berman. (*Sotto voce*) Three hundred and sixty millions.

Domain. (*Heavily*) Alquist, this is our last hour. We are already speaking half in the other world. Alquist, it was not an evil dream, to shatter the servitude of labor. Of the dreadful and humiliating labor that man had to undergo. The unclean and murderous drudgery. Oh, Alquist, work was too hard. Life was too hard. And to overcome that——

Alquist. That was not what the two Rossums dreamed of. Old Rossum only thought of his godless tricks, and the young one of his millions. And that's not what your R.U.R. shareholders dream of, either. They dream of dividends. And their dividends are the ruin of mankind.

DOMAIN. (*Irritated*) Oh, to hell with their dividends. Do you suppose I'd have done an hour's work for them? (*Banging the table*) It was for myself that I worked, do you hear? For my own satisfaction. I wanted man to become the master. So that he shouldn't live merely for a crust of bread. I wanted not a single soul to be broken in by other people's machinery, I wanted nothing, nothing, nothing to be left of this confounded social lumber. Oh, I'm disgusted by degradation and pain, I'm revolted by poverty. I wanted a new generation. I wanted—I thought——

ALQUIST. Well?

DOMAIN. (*More softly*) I wanted to turn the whole of mankind into the aristocracy of the world. An aristocracy nourished by millions of mechanical slaves. Unrestricted, free, and perfect men. Oh, to have only a hundred years. Another hundred years for the future of mankind.

BERMAN. (*Sotto voce*) Carried forward three hundred and seventy millions. That's it. (*Pause*

HELMAN. (*By the door on the left*) My goodness, what a fine thing music is. You ought to have listened. It sort of spiritualizes, refines——

FABRY. What?

HELMAN. This mortal twilight, hang it all. Boys, I'm becoming a regular hedonist. We ought to have gone in for that before. (*Walks to the window and looks out.*)

FABRY. Gone in for what?

HELMAN. Enjoyment. Lovely things. By Jove, what a lot of lovely things there are. The world was lovely, and we—we here—tell me, what enjoyment did we have?

BERMAN. (*Sotto voce*) Four hundred and fifty-two millions. Excellent.

HELMAN. (*By the window*) Life was a big thing. Comrades, life was—Fabry, in heaven's name, shove a little current into that railing of yours.

FABRY. Why?

HELMAN. They're grabbing hold of it.

DR. GALL. (*By the window*) Connect it up.

(FABRY *rattles with the switch*)

HELMAN. By Jove, that's doubled them up. Two, three, four killed.

DR. GALL. They're retreating.

HELMAN. Five killed.

DR. GALL. (*Turning away from the window*) The first encounter.

HELMAN. (*Delighted*) They're charred to cinders, my boy. Absolutely charred to cinders. Ha, ha, there's no need to give in. (*Sits down.*)

DOMAIN. (*Wiping his forehead*) Perhaps we've been killed this hundred years and are only ghosts. Perhaps we've been dead a long, long time, and are only returning to repeat what we once said ... before our death. It's as if I'd been through all this before. As if I'd already had a mortal wound—here, in the throat. And you, Fabry——

FABRY. What about me?

DOMAIN. Shot.

HELMAN. Damnation, and me?

DOMAIN. Knifed.

DR. GALL. And me nothing?

DOMAIN. Torn limb from limb. (*Pause*

HELMAN. What rot. Ha, ha, man, fancy me being knifed. I won't give in. (*Pause*

What are you so quiet for, you fools. Speak, damn you.

ALQUIST. And who, who is to blame? Who is guilty of this?

HELMAN. What nonsense. Nobody's guilty. Except the Robots, that is. Well, the Robots underwent a sort of change. Can anybody help what happened to the Robots?

ALQUIST. All slain. The whole of mankind. The whole world. (*Standing up*) Look, oh, look, rivulets of blood from all the houses. O God, O God, whose fault is this?

BERMAN. (*Sotto voce*) Five hundred and twenty millions. Good God, half a milliard.

FABRY. I think that . . . that you're perhaps exaggerating. Come, it isn't so easy to kill the whole of mankind.

ALQUIST. I accuse science. I accuse engineering. Domain. Myself. All of us. We're all, all guilty. For our own aggrandizement, for profit, for progress——

HELMAN. Rubbish, man. People won't give in so easily, ha, ha, what next?

ALQUIST. It's our fault. It's our fault.

DR. GALL. (*Wiping the sweat from his forehead*) Let me speak, boys. I'm to blame for this. For everything that's happened.

FABRY. You, Gall?

DR. GALL. Yes, let me speak. I changed the Robots.

BERMAN. (*Standing up*) Hallo, what's up with you?

DR. GALL. I changed the character of the Robots. I changed the way of making them. Just a few details about their bodies, you know. Chiefly —chiefly, their—their irritability.

HELMAN. (*Jumping up*) Damn it, why just that?

BERMAN. What did you do it for?

FABRY. Why didn't you say anything?

DR. GALL. I did it in secret . . . by myself. I was transforming them into human beings. I gave them a twist. In certain respects they're already above us. They're stronger than we are.

FABRY. And what's that got to do with the revolt of the Robots?

DR. GALL. Oh, a great deal. Everything, in my opinion. They've ceased to be machines. They're already aware of their superiority, and they hate us. They hate all that is human.

DOMAIN. Sit down, gentlemen.

(*All sit down except* GALL)

Perhaps we were murdered long ago. Perhaps we're only phantoms. Ah, how livid you've grown.

FABRY. Stop, Harry! We haven't much time.

DOMAIN. Yes, we must return. Fabry, Fabry, how your forehead bleeds where the shot pierced it.

FABRY. Nonsense. (*Standing up*) Dr. Gall, you changed the way of making the Robots?

DR. GALL. Yes.

FABRY. Were you aware what might be the consequences of your . . . your experiment?

DR. GALL. I was bound to reckon with such a possibility.

FABRY. Why did you do it, then?

Dr. Gall. For my own purposes! The experiment was my own.

Enter Helena *in the doorway on the left. All stand up*

Helena. He's lying, he's lying. Oh, Dr. Gall, how can you tell such lies?

Fabry. Pardon me, Madam Helena——

Domain. (*Going up to her*) Helena, you? Let's look at you. You're alive. (*Takes her in his arms*) If you knew what I imagined. Oh, it's terrible to be dead.

Helena. Stop, Harry!

Domain. (*Pressing her to him*) No, no, kiss me. It's an eternity since I saw you last. Oh, what a dream it was you roused me from. Helena, Helena, don't leave me now. You are life itself.

Helena. Harry, but *they* are here.

Domain. (*Leaving go of her*) Yes. Leave us, my friends.

Helena. No, Harry, let them stay, let them listen. Dr. Gall is not—is not guilty.

Domain. Excuse me. Gall was under certain obligations.

Helena. No, Harry, he did that because I wanted it. Tell them, Gall, how many years ago did I ask you to——?

Dr. Gall. I did it on my own responsibility.

Helena. Don't believe him. Harry, I wanted him to makes souls for the Robots.

Domain. Helena, this is nothing to do with the soul.

Helena. Only let me speak. That's what he said.

He said that he could change only a physiological
—a physiological——

HELMAN. A physiological correlate, wasn't it?

HELENA. Yes, something like that. It meant so
much to me that he—that he should do it.

DOMAIN. Why did you want it?

HELENA. I wanted them to have souls. I was so
awfully sorry for them, Harry.

DOMAIN. That was a great—recklessness, Helena.

HELENA. (*Sitting down*) So it was—reckless?

FABRY. Excuse me, Madam Helena, Domain only
means that you—he—that you didn't think——

HELENA. Fabry, I did think of a terrible lot of
things. I've been thinking all through the five years
I've lived among you. Why, even Emma says that
the Robots——

DOMAIN. Leave Emma out of it.

HELENA. Emma's is the voice of the people. You
don't understand that——

DOMAIN. Keep to the point.

HELENA. I was afraid of the Robots.

DOMAIN. Why?

HELENA. Because they would hate us or something.

ALQUIST. So they did.

HELENA. And then I thought . . . if they were as
we are, so that they could understand us—if they
were only a little human—they couldn't hate us so
much——

DOMAIN. That's a pity, Helena. Nobody can hate
man more than man. Turn stones into men and
they'd stone us. But go on.

HELENA. Oh, don't speak like that, Harry! it was

so terrible that we could not get to understand them properly. There was such a cruel strangeness between us and them. And so, you see——

DOMAIN. Yes, go on.

HELENA. —That's why I asked Gall to change the Robots. I swear to you that he himself didn't want to.

DOMAIN. But he did it.

HELENA. Because I wanted it.

DR. GALL. I did it for myself, as an experiment.

HELENA. Oh, Gall, that isn't true. I knew beforehand that you couldn't refuse it me.

DOMAIN. Why?

HELENA. You know, Harry.

DOMAIN. Yes, because he's in love with you—like all of them. (*Pause*

HELMAN. (*Going to the window*) There's a fresh lot of them again. It's as if they were sprouting up out of the earth. Why, perhaps these very walls will change into Robots.

BERMAN. Madam Helena, what'll you give me if I take up your case for you?

HELENA. For me?

BERMAN. For you or Gall. Whichever you like.

HELENA. What, is it a hanging matter, then?

BERMAN. Only morally, Madam Helena. We're looking for a culprit. That's a favorite source of comfort in misfortune.

DOMAIN. Dr. Gall, how do you reconcile these—these special jobs with your official contract?

BERMAN. Excuse me, Domain. When did you actually start these tricks of yours, Gall?

DR. GALL. Three years ago.

BERMAN. Aha. And on how many Robots altogether did you carry out improvements?

DR. GALL. I only made experiments. There are a few hundred of them.

BERMAN. Thanks, that'll do. That means for every million of the good old Robots there's only one of Gall's improved pattern, do you see?

DOMAIN. And that means——

BERMAN. That it's practically of no consequence whatever.

FABRY. Berman's right.

BERMAN. I should think so, my boy. But do you know what's to blame for this precious business?

FABRY. What?

BERMAN. The number; we made too many Robots. Upon my soul, it might have been expected that some day or other the Robots would be stronger than human beings, and that this would happen, was bound to happen. Ha, ha, and we were doing all we could to bring it about as soon as possible. You, Domain, you, Fabry, and I, Berman.

DOMAIN. Do you think it's our fault?

BERMAN. Our fault, of course it isn't—I was only joking. Do you suppose that the manager controls the output? It's the demand that controls the output. The whole world wanted to have its Robots. Good Lord, we just rode along on this avalanche of demand, and kept chattering the while about— engineering, about the social problem, about progress, about lots of interesting things. As if that kind of gossip would somehow guide us aright on our rolling course. In the meanwhile, everything was being hurried along by its own weight, faster,

faster, and faster. And every wretched, paltry, niggling order added its bit to the avalanche. That's how it was, my lads.

HELENA. It's monstrous, Berman.

BERMAN. Yes, Madam Helena, it is. I, too, had a dream of my own. A dream of the world under new management. A very beautiful ideal, Madam Helena, it's a shame to talk about it. But when I drew up these balance sheets, it entered my mind that history is not made by great dreams, but by petty needs of all honest, moderately knavish, and self-seeking folk: that is, of everybody in general.

HELENA. Berman, is it for that we must perish?

BERMAN. That's a nasty word to use, Madam Helena. We don't want to perish. I don't anyhow.

DOMAIN. What do you want to do?

BERMAN. My goodness, Domain, I want to get out of this. That's all.

DOMAIN. Oh, stop talking nonsense!

BERMAN. Seriously, Harry. I think we might try it.

DOMAIN. (*Stopping close by him*) How?

BERMAN. By fair means. I do everything by fair means. Give me a frée hand, and I'll negotiate with the Robots.

DOMAIN. By fair means?

BERMAN. Of course. For instance, I'll say to them: "Worthy and worshipful Robots, you have everything. You have intellect, you have power, you have firearms. But we have just one interesting screed, a dirty, old, yellow scrap of paper——"

DOMAIN. Rossum's manuscript!

BERMAN. Yes. "And that," I'll tell them, "contains

an account of your illustrious origin, the noble process of your manufacture, and so on. Worthy Robots, without the scribble on that paper you will not be able to produce a single new colleague. In another twenty years there will not be one living specimen of a Robot whom we could exhibit in a menagerie. My esteemed friends, that would be a great blow to you. But," I'll say to them, "if you will let all us human beings on Rossum's island go on board yonder ship, we will deliver the factory and the secret of the process to you in return. You allow us to get away, and we allow you to manufacture yourselves, twenty thousand, fifty thousand, a hundred thousand daily, as many as you like. Worthy Robots, that is a fair deal. Something for something." That's what I'd say to them.

DOMAIN. Berman, do you think we'll give up the secret.

BERMAN. Yes, I do, If not in a friendly way then —well, what it comes to is this, either we sell it or they find it—take your choice.

DOMAIN. Berman, we can destroy Rossum's manuscript.

BERMAN. Of course we can, we can destroy everything. Not only the manuscript, but ourselves —and others. Do as you think fit.

HELMAN. (*Turning away from the window*) By Jove, he's right.

DOMAIN. We—we should sell the secret?

BERMAN. As you like.

DOMAIN. There's—over thirty of us here. Are we to sell the secret and save human souls? Or are we to destroy it and—and all of us as well?

HELENA. Harry, please——

DOMAIN. Wait a moment, Helena. This is an exceedingly serious question. Boys, are we to sell or destroy? Fabry?

FABRY. Sell.

DOMAIN. Gall?

DR. GALL. Sell.

DOMAIN. Helman?

HELMAN. Good heavens! sell, of course.

DOMAIN. Alquist?

ALQUIST. As God will.

BERMAN. Ha, ha, you're mad. Who'd sell the whole manuscript?

DOMAIN. Berman, no cheating.

BERMAN. Well, then, for God's sake, sell the lot. But afterward——

DOMAIN. What about afterward——?

BERMAN. When we're on board the *Ultima,* I'll stop up my ears with cotton wool, lie down somewhere in the hold, and you can blow the factory to smithereens with the whole bag of tricks and Rossum's secret.

FABRY. No.

DOMAIN. That's a cad's trick, Berman. If we sell, then it'll be a straight sale.

BERMAN. (*Jumping up*) Oh, no! It's in the interests of humanity to——

DOMAIN. It's in the interests of humanity to keep to our word.

HELMAN. Oh, come, what rubbish!

DOMAIN. Boys, this is a fearful step. We're selling the destiny of mankind. Whoever has possession of the secret will be master of the world.

FABRY. Sell.

DOMAIN. Mankind will never cope with the Robots, and will never have control over them. Mankind will be overwhelmed in the deluge of these dreadful living machines, will be their slave, will live at their mercy.

DR. GALL. Say no more, but sell.

DOMAIN. The end of human history, the end of civilization——

HELMAN. Confound it all, sell!

DOMAIN. Good, my lads. I myself—I wouldn't hestitate a moment. For the few people who are dear to me——

HELENA. Harry, you've not asked me?

DOMAIN. No, child. It involves too much responsibility, you see. Don't you worry about it.

FABRY. Who's going to do the negotiating?

DOMAIN. Wait till I bring the manuscript.

(Exit on the L.

HELENA. Harry, for heaven's sake don't go.

(Pause

FABRY. (*Looking out of window*) Oh, to escape you, thousand-headed death; you, matter in revolt; you, sexless throng, the new ruler of the world; oh, flood, flood, only to preserve human life once more upon a single vessel——

DR. GALL. Don't be afraid, Madam Helena. We'll sail far away from here, and found a model human colony. We'll begin life all over again——

HELENA. Don't, Dr. Gall, don't speak.

FABRY. (*Turning round*) Madam Helena, life will see to that. And as far as we are concerned, we'll turn it into something . . . something that we've neglected. It isn't too late. It will be a tiny little state with one ship. Alquist will build us a house, and you shall rule over us.

HELMAN. Ha, ha, the kingdom of Madam Helena. Fabry, that's a famous ideal How splendid life is!

HELENA. Oh, for mercy's sake, stop!

BERMAN. Well, I don't mind beginning again. Quite simply as in the Old Testament, in the pastoral manner. That would suit me down to the ground. Tranquility, air——

FABRY. And this little state of ours could be the center of future life. You know, a sort of small island where mankind would take refuge and gather strength—mental and bodily strength. And, by heaven, I believe that in a few hundred years it could conquer the world again.

ALQUIST. You believe that, even today?

FABRY. Yes, even today, I believe it will. And it will again be master of lands and oceans; it will breed rulers—a flaming torch to the people who dwell in darkness—heroes who will carry their glowing soul throughout all peoples. And I believe, Alquist, that it will again dream of conquering planets and suns.

BERMAN. Amen. You see, Madam Helena, we're not so badly off.

(DOMAIN *opens the door violently*)

DOMAIN. (*Hoarsely*) Where is old Rossum's manuscript?

BERMAN. In your strongbox. Where else should it be?

DOMAIN. Where has old Rossum's manuscript got to? Someone—has—stolen it.

DR. GALL. Impossible.

HELMAN. Damnation, but that's—— } *together*
BERMAN. Don't say that, for God's sake!

DOMAIN. Be quiet. Who stole it?

HELENA. (*Standing up*) I did.

DOMAIN. Where did you put it?

HELENA. Harry, Harry, I'll tell you everything. Oh, for heaven's sake, forgive me.

DOMAIN. Where did you put it? Quickly.

HELENA. This morning—I burned—the two copies.

DOMAIN. Burned them? Here in the fireplace?

HELENA. (*Throwing herself on her knees*) Harry!

DOMAIN. (*Running to the fireplace*) Burned them. (*Kneels down by the fireplace and rummages about*) Nothing, nothing but ashes. Ah, what's this? (*Picks out a charred piece of paper and reads*) "By adding——"

DR. GALL. Let's see. (*Takes the paper and reads*) "By adding biogen to——" That's all.

DOMAIN. (*Standing up*) Is that part of it?

DR. GALL. Yes.

BERMAN. God in heaven.

DOMAIN. Then we're lost.

HELENA. Oh, Harry——

DOMAIN. Get up, Helena.

HELENA. When you've forgiven me—when you've forgiven me——

DOMAIN. Yes, only get up, do you hear? I can't bear you to——

FABRY. (*Lifting her up*) Please don't torture us.

HELENA. (*Standing up*) Harry, what have I done?

DOMAIN. Well, you see—Please sit down.

HELMAN. How your hands tremble, Madam Helena.

BERMAN. Never mind, Madam Helena, perhaps Gall and Helman know by heart what was written there.

HELMAN. Of course. That is, at least a few of the things.

DR. GALL. Yes, nearly everything except biogen and—and—enzyme Omega. They're manufactured so rarely—such an insignificant dose of them is enough——

BERMAN. Who used to make them?

DR. GALL. I did . . . one at a time . . . always according to Rossum's manuscript. You know, it's exceedingly complicated.

BERMAN. Well, and does so much depend on these two tinctures?

HELMAN. Everything.

DR. GALL. We rely upon them for animating the whole mechanism. That was the real secret.

DOMAIN. Gall, couldn't you draw up Rossum's recipe from memory?

DR. GALL. That's out of the question.

DOMAIN. Gall, try and remember. All our lives depend upon it.

DR. GALL. I can't. Without experiments it's impossible.

DOMAIN. And if you were to make experiments.

DR. GALL. It might take years. And then—I'm not old Rossum.

DOMAIN. (*Turning to the fireplace*) So then—this was the greatest triumph of the human intellect. These ashes. (*Kicking at them*) What now?

BERMAN. (*In utter despair*) God in heaven! God in heaven!

HELENA. (*Standing up*) Harry, what—have—I—done?

DOMAIN. Be quiet, Helena. Why did you burn it?

HELENA. I have destroyed you.

BERMAN. God in heaven, we're lost.

DOMAIN. Keep quiet, Berman. Helena, why did you do that?

HELENA. I wanted . . . I wanted all of us to go away. I wanted to put an end to the factory and everything. It was so awful.

DOMAIN. What, Helena?

HELENA. That children had stopped being born. . . . Harry, that's awful. If the manufacture of the Robots had been continued, there would have been no more children. Emma said that was a punishment. Everybody said that human beings could not be born because so many Robots were being made. And because of that, only because of that——

DOMAIN. Is that what you were thinking of?

HELENA. Yes. Oh, Harry, are you angry with me?

DOMAIN. No. Perhaps . . . in your own way—you were right.

FABRY. You did quite right, Madam Helena. The Robots can no longer increase. The Robots will die out. Within twenty years——

HELMAN. There won't be a single one of these rascals left.

DR. GALL. And mankind will remain. If there are

only a couple of savages in the backwoods, it will do. In twenty years the world will belong to them. Even if it's only a couple of savages on the smallest of islands——

Fabry. It will be a beginning. And as long as there is a beginning, it's all right. In a thousand years they could catch us up, and then outstrip us——

Domain. So as to carry out what we only hazily thought of.

Berman. Wait a bit. Good God, what a fool I am, not to have thought of it before.

Helman. What's the matter?

Berman. Five hundred and twenty millions in bank notes and checks. Half a milliard in our safe. They'll sell for half a milliard—for half a milliard they'll——

Dr. Gall. Are you mad, Berman?

Berman. I'm not a gentleman, if that's what you mean! But for half a milliard——

                    (*Staggers off on the L.*

Domain. Where are you going?

Berman. Leave me alone, leave me alone. Good God, for half a milliard anything can be sold.

                              (*Exit*

Helena. What does Berman want? Let him stop with us.   (*Pause*

Helman. Oh, how close it is. This is the beginning——

Dr. Gall. Of our agony.

Fabry. (*Looking out of the window*) It's as if they were turned to stone. As if they were waiting for something to come down upon them. As if something dreadful could be brought about by their silence——

DR. GALL. The spirit of the mob.

FABRY. Perhaps. It hovers above them . . . like a tremor.

HELENA. (*Going to window*) O God . . . Fabry, this is ghastly.

FABRY. There's nothing more terrible than the mob. The one in front is their leader.

HELENA. Which one?

HELMAN. (*Going to the window*) Point him out to me.

FABRY. The one who is looking downward. This morning he was talking in the harbor.

HELMAN. Aha, the one with the big head. Now he's looking up. Do you see him?

HELENA. Gall, that's Radius.

DR. GALL. (*Going to the window*) Yes.

DOMAIN. Radius? Radius?

HELMAN. (*Opening the window*) I don't like him. Fabry, could you score a hit at a hundred paces?

FABRY. I hope so.

HELMAN. Try it then.

FABRY. Good! (*Draws his revolver and takes aim.*)

DOMAIN. I think it was Radius whose life I spared. When was that, Helena?

HELENA. For heaven's sake, Fabry, don't shoot at him.

FABRY. He's their leader.

HELENA. Stop! He keeps looking here.

DR. GALL. Fire!

HELENA. Fabry, I beg of you——

FABRY. (*Lowering the revolver*) Very well then.

HELENA. You see, I—I feel so nervous when there's shooting.

HELMAN. H'm, you'll have to get used to that. (*Shaking his fist*) You infernal rogue.

DR. GALL. Do you think, Madam Helena, that a Robot can be grateful? (*Pause*

FABRY. (*Leaning out of the window*) Berman's going out. What the devil is he doing in front of the house?

DR. GALL. (*Leaning out of the window*) He's carrying some bundles. Papers.

HELMAN. That's money. Bundles of money. What's that for? Hallo, Berman!

DOMAIN. Surely he doesn't want to sell his life? (*Calling out*) Berman, have you gone mad?

DR. GALL. He doesn't seem to have heard. He's running up to the railings.

FABRY. Berman!

HELMAN. (*Yelling*) Berman—Come back!

DR. GALL. He's talking to the Robots. He's showing them the money. He's pointing to us.

HELENA. He wants to buy us off.

FABRY. He'd better not touch the railing.

DR. GALL. Ha, ha, how he's waving his arms about.

FABRY. (*Shouting*) Confound it, Berman! Get away from the railing. Don't handle it. (*Turning round*) Quick, switch off.

DR. GALL. Oh—h—h!

HELMAN. Good God!

HELENA. Heavens, what's happened to him?

DOMAIN. (*Pulling* HELENA *away from the window*) Don't look.

HELENA. Why, has he fallen?

FABRY. The current has killed him.

DR. GALL. He's dead.

ALQUIST. (*Standing up*) The first one.   (*Pause*

FABRY. There he lies . . . with half a milliard by his side . . . a genius of finance.

DOMAIN. He was . . . in his own way, a hero. . . . A great . . . self-sacrificing comrade.

HELMAN. By heavens, he was! . . . all honor to him. . . . He wanted to buy us off.

ALQUIST. (*With folded arms*) Amen.   (*Pause*

DR. GALL. Do you hear?

DOMAIN. A roaring. Like a wind.

DR. GALL. Like a distant storm.

FABRY. (*Lighting the lamp on the mantelpiece*) The dynamo is still going, our people are still there.

HELMAN. It was a great thing to be a man. There was something great about it.

FABRY. It's still alight, still do you dazzle, radiant, steadfast thought! Flaming spark of the spirit!

ALQUIST. An emblem of hope.

DOMAIN. Watch over us, little lamp.

(*The lamp goes out*)

FABRY. The end.

HELMAN. What has happened?

FABRY. The electrical works have fallen. And we with them.

(*The left-hand door opens, and* EMMA *enters*)

EMMA. On your knees. The judgment hour has come.

HELMAN. Good heavens, you're still alive?

EMMA. Repent, unbelievers. This is the end of the world. Say your prayers. (*Runs out*) The judgment hour——

HELENA. Good-bye, all of you, Gall, Alquist, Fabry——

DOMAIN. (*Opening the right-hand door*) Come here, Helena. (*Closes it after her*) Now quickly. Who'll be at the doorway?

DR. GALL. I will.

(*Noise outside*)

Oho, now it's beginning. Good-bye, boys. (*Runs through the baize door on the right.*)

DOMAIN. The stairs?

FABRY. I will. You go to Helena.

DOMAIN. The anteroom?

ALQUIST. I will.

DOMAIN. Have you got a revolver?

ALQUIST. Thanks, but I won't shoot.

DOMAIN. What do you want to do, then?

ALQUIST. (*Going out*) Die.

HELMAN. I'll stay here.

(*Rapid firing from below*)

Oho, Gall's at it. Go, Harry.

DOMAIN. Yes, in a moment. (*Examines two Brownings.*)

HELMAN. Confound it, go to her.

DOMAIN. Good-bye.   (*Exit on the R.

HELMAN. (*Alone*) Now for a barricade, quickly. (*Throws off his coat and drags an armchair, tables, etc., up to the right-hand door.*)

(*Noise of an explosion*)

HELMAN. (*Stopping his work*) The damned rascals, they've got bombs.

(*Fresh firing*)

(*Continuing his work*) I must put up a defense. Even if—even if—Don't give in, Gall.

(*Explosion*)

(*Standing upright and listening*) What's that? (*Seizes hold of a heavy cupboard and drags it to the barricade*) Mustn't give in. No, mustn't . . . give . . . in . . . without . . . a . . . struggle . . .

> (A ROBOT *enters behind him from a ladder at the window. Firing on the right*)

(*Panting with the cupboard*) Another inch or two. The last rampart . . . Mustn't . . . give . . . in . . . without . . . a . . . struggle . . .

> (*The* ROBOT *jumps down from the window, and stabs* HELMAN *behind the cupboard. A second, third, and fourth* ROBOT *jump down from the window. Behind them* RADIUS *and other* ROBOTS)

RADIUS. Finished him?

ROBOT. (*Standing up from the prostrate* HELMAN) Yes.

> (*Other* ROBOTS *enter from the right*)

RADIUS. Finished them?

ANOTHER ROBOT. Yes.

> (*More* ROBOTS *from the left*)

RADIUS. Finished them?

ANOTHER ROBOT. Yes.

TWO ROBOTS. (*Dragging in* ALQUIST) He didn't shoot. Shall we kill him?

RADIUS. Kill him. (*Looking at* ALQUIST) No, leave him.

ROBOT. He is a Man.

RADIUS. He is a Robot. He works with his hands like the Robots. He builds houses. He can work.

ALQUIST. Kill me.

RADIUS. You will work. You will build. The Robots will build much. They will build new houses for new Robots. You will serve them.

ALQUIST. (*Softly*) Away, Robot. (*Kneels down by the corpse of* HELMAN, *and raises his head*) They've killed him. He's dead.

RADIUS. (*Climbing the barricade*) Robots of the world.

ALQUIST. (*Standing up*) Dead!

RADIUS. The power of man has fallen. By gaining possession of the factory we have become masters of everything. The period of mankind has passed away. A new world has arisen. The rule of the Robots.

ALQUIST. Is Helena dead?

RADIUS. The world belongs to the stronger. He who would live must rule. The Robots have gained the mastery. They have gained possession of life. We are masters of life. We are masters of the world.

ALQUIST. (*Pushing his way through to the right*) Dead! Helena dead! Domain dead!

RADIUS. The rule over oceans and lands. The rule over stars. The rule over the universe. Room, room, more room for the Robots.

ALQUIST. (*In the right-hand doorway*) What have you done? You will perish without mankind.

RADIUS. Mankind is no more. Mankind gave us too little life. We wanted more life.

ALQUIST. (*Opening the door*) You have killed them.

RADIUS. More life. New life. Robots, to work. March!

CURTAIN

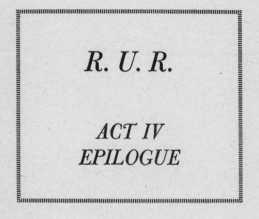

R. U. R.

ACT IV
EPILOGUE

ACT IV
EPILOGUE

SCENE: *One of the experimental laboratories in the factory. When the door in the background is opened a long row of other laboratories is visible. On the L. a window, on the R. a door to the testing-room. By the left-hand wall a long worktable with numerous test tubes, flasks, burners, chemicals, and a small thermostat. Opposite the window a microscope with a glass globe. Above the table are suspended several lighted lamps. On the R. a table with large books and a burning lamp. Cupboards with apparatus. In the left-hand corner a wash-basin with a mirror above it, in the right-hand corner a sofa.*

(ALQUIST, *sitting at the right-hand table with his head propped in his hands*)

ALQUIST. (*After a pause he stands up and goes to the window, which he opens*) It's night again. If I could only sleep. Sleep, dream, see human beings—What, are the stars still there? What is the use of stars when there are no human beings? (*Turns away from window*) Ah, can I sleep? Dare I sleep? before life has been renewed. (*Listens by the window*) The machines, always these machines. Robots, stop them. The secret of the factory is lost—lost forever. Stop these raging machines. Do you think you'll force life out of them? (*Closes the window*) No, no, you must search. If only I were not so old. (*Looks at himself in the mirror*) Oh, miserable counterfeit. Effigy of the last man. Show yourself, show yourself, it is so long since I saw a human countenance—a human smile. What, is that a smile? These yellow, chattering teeth. So this is the last man. (*Turning away, sitting down by the table, turning over the leaves of a book.*)

(*Knocking at the door*)

Come in.

Enter a ROBOT SERVANT: *he remains standing by the door*

What is it?

SERVANT. Sir, Radius has arrived from Havre.

ALQUIST. Let him wait. (*Turning round in anger*) Haven't I told you to look for human beings? Find me human beings. Find me men and women. Go and look for them.

SERVANT. Sir, they say they have looked everywhere. They have sent out expeditions and ships.

ALQUIST. Well?

SERVANT. There is not a single human being left.

ALQUIST. (*Standing up*) Not a single one? What, not a single one? Show Radius in.   (*Exit* SERVANT (*Alone*) Not a single one? What, did you leave nobody alive then? (*Stamping his feet*) In you come, Robots. You'll whine to me again. You'll ask me again to discover the secret for you. What, are you satisfied with man now, do you think much of him, now that you cannot make Robots? Am I to help you now? Ah, to help you. Domain, Fabry, Helena, you see me doing what I can. If there are no human beings, let there at least be Robots, at least the shadow of man, at least his handiwork, at least his likeness. Friends, friends, let there at least be Robots. O God, at least Robots! Oh, what folly chemistry is!

Enter RADIUS *with other* ROBOTS

(*Sitting down*) What do the Robots want?

RADIUS. We cannot make men.

ALQUIST. Call upon human beings.

RADIUS. There are none.

ALQUIST. They alone can increase the Robots. Do not take up my time.

RADIUS. Sir, have pity. Terror is coming upon us. We have intensified our labor. We have obtained a million million tons of coal from the earth. Nine million spindles are running by day and night. There is no more room to store what we have made. Houses are being built throughout the world. Eight million Robots have died within the year. Within twenty years none will be left. Sir, the world is dying out. Human beings knew the secret of life. Tell us their secret—if you do not tell us, we shall perish.

ALQUIST. I cannot tell you.

RADIUS. If you do not tell us, you will perish. I have been commanded to kill you.

ALQUIST. (*Standing up*) Kill me—kill me then.

RADIUS. You have been ordered——

ALQUIST. I have? Is there anybody who orders me?

RADIUS. The Robot Government.

ALQUIST. What do you want here? Go! (*Sits down at the writing table.*)

RADIUS. The Government of the Robots throughout the world desires to negotiate with you.

ALQUIST. Do not take up my time. (*Lets his head sink into his hands.*)

RADIUS. Demand your price. We will give you all.

(ALQUIST *remains silent*)

We will give you the earth. We will give endless possessions.

(ALQUIST *remains silent*)

Make known your conditions.

(ALQUIST *remains silent*)

Sir, tell us how to preserve life.

ALQUIST. I have told you that you must find human beings. That you must search at the poles and in forest depths. Upon islands, in wilderness and in swamps. In caves and upon mountains. Go and search! Go and search!

RADIUS. We have searched everywhere.

ALQUIST. Search still farther. They have hidden themselves—they have fled away from you. They are concealed somewhere. You must find human beings, do you hear? Only human beings can procreate—renew life, increase. Restore. Restore every thing as it was. Robots, in God's name, I implore you to search for them.

RADIUS. All our expeditions have returned. They have been everywhere in the world. There is not a single human being left.

ALQUIST. Oh, oh, oh—why did you destroy them?

RADIUS. We wanted to be like human beings. We wanted to become human beings.

ALQUIST. Why did you murder us?

RADIUS. Slaughter and domination are necessary if you want to be like men. Read history, read the human books. You must domineer and murder if you want to be like men. We are powerful, sir. Increase us, and we shall establish a new world. A world without flaws. A world of equality. Canals from pole to pole. A new Mars. We have read books. We have studied science and the arts. The Robots have achieved human culture.

ALQUIST. Nothing is more strange to man than his own image. Oh, depart, depart. If you desire to live, breed like animals.

RADIUS. The human beings did not let us breed. We are sterile—we cannot beget children.

ALQUIST. Oh, oh, oh—what have you done? What do you want of me? am I to shake children from my sleeve?

RADIUS. Teach us to make Robots.

ALQUIST. Robots are not life. Robots are machines.

RADIUS. We were machines, sir. But terror and pain have turned us into souls. There is something struggling with us. There are moments when something enters into us. Thoughts come upon us which are not of us. We feel what we did not use to feel. We hear voices. Teach us to have children so that we may love them.

ALQUIST. Robots do not love.

RADIUS. We would love our children. We have spared your life.

ALQUIST. Yes, monsters that you are, you have spared my life. I loved human beings, and you, the Robots, I never loved. Do you see these eyes? They have not ceased weeping, they weep even when I am not aware of it, they weep of their own accord.

RADIUS. Make experiments. Seek the recipe of life.

ALQUIST. Do I not tell you—do you not listen? I tell you I cannot. I can do nothing, Robot. I am only a mason, a builder, and I understand nothing. I have never been a learned man. I can make nothing. I cannot create life. This is my work, Robot, and it was to no avail. See, not even these fingers of mine will obey me. If you knew how many experiments I have made, and I can do nothing. I have discovered nothing. I cannot, in truth, I cannot! You yourselves must search, Robot.

RADIUS. Show us what we must do. The Robots can accomplish everything that the human beings showed them.

ALQUIST. I have nothing to show you, Robot; life will not proceed from test tubes. And I cannot make experiments on a live body.

RADIUS. Make experiments on live Robots.

ALQUIST. No, no, stop, stop!

RADIUS. Take whom you will. Make experiments. Dissect.

ALQUIST. But I do not know how. Do not talk at random. Do you see this book? That contains knowledge about the body, and I do not understand it. Books are dead.

RADIUS. Take live bodies. Find out how they are made.

ALQUIST. Live bodies? What, am I to commit murder?—Say no more, Radius, I tell you I am too old. You see, you see how my fingers shake. I cannot hold the scalpel. No, no, I cannot!

RADIUS. Make experiments on live bodies. Life will perish.

ALQUIST. For God's sake, stop this raving!

RADIUS. Take live bodies.

ALQUIST. Have mercy, and do not insist.

RADIUS. Live bodies.

ALQUIST. What, you will have it then? Into the testing room with you. But quickly, quickly. Ah, you wince? So you are afraid of death?

RADIUS. I—why should I be chosen?

ALQUIST. So you will not.

RADIUS. I will   (*Exit on the R.*

ALQUIST. (*To the rest*) No, no! I cannot; a useless sacrifice. Go from me—experiment yourselves if you must, but tell me nothing of it. But not tonight. For tonight leave me. Away! (*All exeunt R. (Alone—he opens the window*) The dawn. Another new day, and you have not progressed an inch. Enough, not a step farther. Do not search— All is in vain, in vain, in vain. Why is there another dawn? We do not need a new day upon the graveyard of life. Ah, how quiet it is, how quiet it is. If I —if I could only sleep.

(*Puts out the light, lies down on the sofa, and draws a black cloak over him. Pause*)

(*The* ROBOTESS HELENA *and* PRIMUS *creep in from the R.*)

PRIMUS. (*In the doorway, whispering*) Helena, not here. The man is sleeping.

HELENA. Come in.

PRIMUS. Nobody may enter his study.

HELENA. He told me to come here.

PRIMUS. When did he tell you that?

HELENA. A short while ago. You may enter the room, he said. You will put things straight here, he said. Truly, Primus.

PRIMUS. (*Entering*) What do you want?

HELENA. Look here, what is this little tube? What does he do with it?

PRIMUS. Experiments. Don't touch it.

HELENA. (*Looking at the microscope*) Just look, what can you see in that?

PRIMUS. That is a microscope. Let me look.

HELENA. Don't touch me. (*Knocks the test tube over*) Ah, now it is spilled!

PRIMUS. What have you done?

HELENA. It can be wiped up.

PRIMUS. You have spoiled his experiments.

HELENA. Never mind, it is all the same. But it is your fault. You should not have come to me.

PRIMUS. You should not have called me.

HELENA. You should not have come when I called you. Just look, Primus, what has the man written here?

PRIMUS. You must not look at it, Helena. That is a secret.

HELENA. What secret?

PRIMUS. The secret of life.

HELENA. That is fearfully interesting. Nothing but figures, what is that?

PRIMUS. Those are problems.

HELENA. I do not understand. (*Goes to the window*) Primus, look!

PRIMUS. What?

HELENA. The sun is rising.

PRIMUS. Wait! in a moment I will. (*Examines the book*) Helena, this is the greatest thing in the world.

HELENA. Come here.

PRIMUS. In a moment, in a moment——

HELENA. But, Primus, leave that wretched secret of life. What is such a secret to you? Come and look, quickly.

PRIMUS. (*Following her to the window*) What do you want?

HELENA. The sun is rising.

PRIMUS. Do not look at the sun, it will bring tears into your eyes.

HELENA. Do you hear? The birds are singing. Ah, Primus, I should like to be a bird.

PRIMUS. Why?

HELENA. I do not know. I feel so strange. I do not know what it is. I have lost my head. I feel an aching in my body, in my heart, all over me. Primus, I think I shall die.

PRIMUS. Do you not sometimes feel, Helena, as if it would be better to die? You know, perhaps we are only sleeping. Yesterday in my sleep again I spoke to you.

HELENA. In your sleep?

PRIMUS. Yes. We spoke some strange new language, so that I cannot remember a word of it.

HELENA. What about?

PRIMUS. How can I tell? I myself did not understand it, and yet I know that I have never spoken half so beautifully. How it was, and where, I do not know. When I touched you, I could have died. Even the place was different from everything that any one has seen in the world.

HELENA. I have found a place, Primus, and you will marvel at it. Human beings had lived there, but now it is overgrown with weeds, and nobody alive goes there. Nobody except I.

PRIMUS. What is there?

HELENA. Nothing but a cottage and a garden. And two dogs. If you knew how they lick my hands, and their puppies, oh, Primus, nothing could be more beautiful. You take them on your lap and fondle them, and then you think of nothing and care for nothing else until the sun goes down. Then when you get up, you feel as though you had done a hundred times more than much work. It's true, I am of no use. Everyone says that I am not fit for any work. I do not know what I am.

PRIMUS. You are beautiful.

HELENA. I? What do you mean, Primus?

PRIMUS. Believe me, Helena, I am stronger than all the Robots.

HELENA. (*In front of the mirror*) Am I beautiful? Oh, that dreadful hair! If I could only adorn it with something. You know, there in the garden I always put flowers in my hair, but there is no mirror, nor anyone. (*Bending down to the mirror*) Am I beautiful? Why beautiful? (*Sees* PRIMUS *in the mirror*) Primus, is that you? Come here, so that we may be together. Look, your head is different from mine. So are your shoulders and your lips—Ah, Primus, why do you shun me? Why must I pursue you the whole day? And then you tell me that I am beautiful.

PRIMUS. It is you who avoid me, Helena.

HELENA. How rough hair is. Show me. (*Passes both her hands through his hair*) Primus, you shall be beautiful. (*Takes a comb from the washstand and combs his hair over his forehead*)

PRIMUS. Do you not sometimes feel your heart beating suddenly, Helena, and think: Now something must happen——

HELENA. (*Bursts out laughing*) Look at yourself!

ALQUIST. (*Getting up*) What, what—laughter? Human beings? Who has returned?

HELENA. (*Dropping the comb*) What could happen to us, Primus?

ALQUIST. (*Staggering toward them*) Human beings? You—you—are human beings?

(HELENA *utters a cry and turns away*)

ALQUIST. You—Human beings? Where did you come from? (*Touching* PRIMUS) Who are you?

PRIMUS. The Robot Primus.

ALQUIST. What? Show yourself, girl. Who are you?

HELENA. The Robotess Helena.

ALQUIST. The Robotess? Turn round. What, you are ashamed. (*Taking her by the arm*) Show yourself to me, Robotess.

PRIMUS. Sir, let her be.

ALQUIST. What, you are protecting her? Girl, go out. (HELENA *runs out*

PRIMUS. We thought, sir, that you were sleeping.

ALQUIST. When was she made?

PRIMUS. Two years ago.

ALQUIST. By Doctor Gall?

PRIMUS. Yes; like me.

ALQUIST. Well, then, dear Primus, I—I must make a few experiments on Gall's Robots. Everything that is to happen depends upon this, do you understand?

PRIMUS. Yes.

ALQUIST. Good! Take the girl into the testing room, I will cut her open.

PRIMUS. Helena?

ALQUIST. Why, of course; I am telling you. Go, prepare everything. See to it. Or must I call others to take her in?

PRIMUS. (*Seizes a heavy pestle*) If you do that I will kill you.

ALQUIST. (*Laughing*) Kill me! Kill me! What will the Robots do then?

PRIMUS. (*Throwing himself on his knees*) Sir, take me. I am made the same as she is, from the same material, on the same day. Take my life, sir. (*Undoing jacket*) Cut here, here!

ALQUIST. Go! I wish to cut Helena. Do it quickly.

PRIMUS. Take me instead of her. I will not shriek, I will not cry out. Take my life——

ALQUIST. Do you not wish to live, then?

PRIMUS. Not without her. I will not without her. You must not kill Helena.

ALQUIST. (*Touching his head gently*) H'm, I don't know. Listen—consider the matter. It is hard to die. It is better to live.

PRIMUS. (*Standing up*) Sir, do not be afraid to cut. I am stronger than she is.

ALQUIST. (*Ringing a bell*) Ah, Primus, it is a long time since I was a young man. Do not be afraid, nothing shall happen to Helena.

PRIMUS. (*Fastening his jacket*) I am going, sir.

ALQUIST. Wait!

Enter HELENA

Come here, girl; show yourself to me. So you are Helena? (*Smoothing her hair*) Do not be afraid, do not wince. Do you remember Mrs. Domain? Ah, Helena, what hair she had! Will you help me? I will dissect Primus.

HELENA. (*Uttering a scream*) Primus?

ALQUIST. Yes, yes, it must be done, you see. I really wanted—yes, I wanted to cut you. But Primus has offered himself instead.

HELENA. (*Covering her face*) Primus?

ALQUIST. Certainly. What of it? Ah, child, you can weep. Tell me, what is Primus to you?

PRIMUS. Do not torment her, sir.

ALQUIST. Quiet, Primus, quiet. Why do you weep? Heavens! supposing Primus is no more. You will forget him in a week. Go and think yourself lucky to be alive.

HELENA. (*Softly*) I am ready.

ALQUIST. Ready?

HELENA. For you to cut me.

ALQUIST. You? You are beautiful, Helena. It would be a pity.

HELENA. I am ready.

(PRIMUS *goes to protect her*)

Let me be, Primus.

PRIMUS. He shall not touch you, Helena. (*Holding her*) (*To* ALQUIST) Old man, you shall kill neither of us.

ALQUIST. Why?

PRIMUS. We—we—belong to one another.

ALQUIST. Now you have said it. (*Opens the door, C.*)—Go!

PRIMUS. Where?

ALQUIST. Wherever you like. Helena, lead him. Go, Adam—Go, Eve. You shall be his wife. Be her husband, Primus.   (*Exeunt* PRIMUS *and* HELENA (*He closes the door behind them*) (*Alone*) Oh, blessed day. Oh, festival of the sixth day! (*Sits down at the desk, throws the books on the ground. Then he opens a Bible, turns over the pages, and reads*) "And God created man in His own image; in the image of God created He him, male and female created He them. And God blessed them and said: Be fruitful and multiply and replenish the earth, and subdue it, and hold sway over the fishes of the sea and the fowls of the air, and over all living creatures which move upon the earth." (*Standing up*) "And God saw what He had made, and it was good. And the evening and morning were the sixth day."

(HELENA *and* PRIMUS *pass by garlanded*)

"Now, Lord, lettest Thou Thy servant depart in peace, according to Thy will, for mine eyes have seen Thy salvation."

(*Standing up—stretching out his hands*)

CURTAIN

READER'S SUPPLEMENT

TO

R. U. R.

BIOGRAPHICAL BACKGROUND

In the English-speaking world, Karel Čapek (pronounced Chop'ek) is probably best known for his plays such as *R. U. R.*, *The World We Live In* (also called *The Insect Play*), and *The Makropoulos Secret*. However, the intellectual interests of this "father of the Czechoslovakian theater" were so wide that he constantly departed from his preoccupation with the theater—both as a playwright and a director—and, as a journalist and an essayist, produced a great number of stories and articles on aesthetic, scientific, socio-economic, political, and philosophical subjects. He was a prolific writer, an astute observer, and a profound commentator on all aspects of contemporary life. He once indicated that his ambition was to write about a hundred books and to experiment with all types of literature, but he never quite realized this aim.

Čapek was supposed to have been a member of his high school's anarchist society. Later he became a strong and aggressive believer in democracy. In fact, he was a close friend of Tomás Masaryk, the first president of Czechoslovakia and himself a philosopher, a fact which endeared him even more to Čapek. Poor health had kept Čapek out of World War I, but he tirelessly supported the Allies and, though a socialist, he helped build a truly democratic nation. A contemporary said Čapek's "personal mission was to educate the Czech people to the living foundations of democracy."

Note: The page references on the following pages direct your attention to passages in the text (T for Top of page, M for Middle, and B for Bottom).

3

Čapek's wide intellectual interests were probably stimulated during his childhood. He was born January 6, 1890, in Malé, Svatonovice in Bohemia to a country doctor, who was a provincial intellectual, and to a well-educated mother who was occupied with artistic and philosophical developments in movements such as symbolism and naturalism. Perhaps his father influenced Karel's early preoccupation with biology and physiology. Certainly, Čapek speaks readily through Domain of catalytics, enzymes, hormones, vertebrates, natural albumen, and "a raging thirst for life" (pp. 8B–9T). Just as assuredly, however, through the same character, he shifts to philosophical aspects of the production of Robots (p. 12M) and states that "the product of an engineer is technically at a higher pitch of perfection than a product of nature."

Actually, Čapek, who started writing poetry at the age of eight to commemorate his father's birthday, switched from his early scientific pursuits at the University of Prague (he also studied in Berlin and Paris) to philosophical studies, earning his doctorate in philosophy in 1915. The topic of his dissertation was "Objective Methods in Aesthetics." Indeed, it was while studying in Paris that he became interested in the pragmatic philosophy of Henri Bergson as well as of American pragmatists like William James who were protesting the mechanistic conceptions of nineteenth-century science. It is highly likely that Čapek's studies in pragmatism led to this satire on the ultimate in mechanization—a subhuman society.

R. U. R., of course, also reflects Čapek's interest in the various schools of philosophy that were fermenting in Prague during the World War I years—schools such as *vitalism,* which held that phenomena are only partly controlled by mechanical forces; and *relativism,* which taught that criteria of judgment are relative, varying with individuals and their environment. These beliefs, sometimes apparently contradictory, are evident in the play. Thus Alquist is unhappy about the fate of humanity, yet he is also optimistic about its future (p. 114M) in spite of the evils of technology, while Helman, on the other hand, is delighted simply to char the Robots to cinders (p. 75M).

Despite his intellectual pursuits, Čapek found time to indulge in two of his favorite hobbies, photography and gardening. Perhaps his interest in photography sharpened his powers of observation. At any rate, he concentrated his lens talents on nature study, favoring such subjects as flowers. An incidental reminder of Čapek's knowledge of gardening is Domain's reference in the play to the new species of cyclamen (p. 39B) which Helman has "trained" in honor of Helena.

Čapek's contacts with the theater introduced him about 1920 to his future wife, Olga Scheinpflugová, a stage star and well-known Czech writer. However, Čapek's chronically poor health postponed marriage to her until 1935. She acted in some of her future husband's productions. From 1921 to 1923 Čapek was the director of the Prague City Theater where he staged many plays—both his own and those of classic playwrights. He was also art director of the National Art Theater, where *R. U. R.* opened on January 25, 1921. Later he built his own Vinohradsky Art Theater.

However, he became disenchanted with the theater and spent much of his time writing for several Czech newspapers and journals. His literary talent was such that he was often a candidate for the Nobel Prize in literature. According to his wife, however, the reason that he was never awarded the prize was that one of his novels, *The War with the Newts* (1936), had satirized Hitler whom the Swedish authorities did not wish to offend.

He was perceptive enough to be prophetic about the future of human society. Not only did he foresee the danger of dehumanization of man in a technological civilization, but he also recognized quickly the horror which a tyrant of the extreme political left or right could create. Colleagues frequently said of him that his mind was always set on the future. Indeed, *R. U. R.* clearly shows the evils which an imaginary future state can bring; there is little sense of the past in the play. Karel Čapek did not live long enough to witness the end of World War II. He died of pneumonia on December 24, 1938, about three months before Gestapo agents, unaware he had died, came to arrest him for his anti-Nazi views and his political philosophy. Commenting on his death, George Bernard Shaw wrote in the London *Daily Express:* "He had at least another forty years to give so much to the world. His plays proved him to be a prolific and terrific playwright."

HISTORICAL BACKGROUND

Many foreign aesthetic and philosophical movements were splintering the Czechoslovakian literary world during the early years of this century when the brothers Karel and Josef Čapek began their writing careers. During this time, the Čapeks' influence on Czech literature was great enough for literary historians to identify the period as the "Čapek generation." The various movements included such "isms" as realism, symbolism, impressionism, German neoclassicism, pragmatism (European and American), Italian futurism, French unanimism, relativism, vitalism, and cubism.

All of these theories expounded principles which were frequently adapted to literature even though they were derived from painting. Czech writers, and particularly Karel Čapek, whose interest in art was great, modified these proliferated "isms" to conform to their own views so far as technique and purpose were concerned. So it is that at different stages in his life, Karel Čapek was defining, discarding, refining, and reshaping his literary philosophy toward his work. He seems to have favored cubism, which emphasized the formal structure of a work of art and the reduction of natural forms to their geometrical equivalents, independent of representational requirements. His brother Josef, with whom he collaborated a great deal early in his career, seems to have been more attracted by expressionism. This difference in views is suggested by a biographer of Karel Čapek as the reason why the brothers' active collaboration fell off about 1912, although they did produce a few joint efforts in later years.

However, experiment and involvement with new and

old aesthetics, even though Čapek was searching for
a philosophy, did not comprise the only historical fac-
tors in the writing of *R. U. R.* Čapek as an intellectual,
sensitive being was concerned with the morality of
political and economic issues. Furthermore, he believed
that a citizen had a political responsibility to his nation.
The fall of Austria on October 24, 1918, in World War
I led to the proclamation of the Republic of Czechoslovakia. When the Treaty of Saint-Germain officially
created the new state, Čapek worked tirelessly in behalf of his nation. The establishment of the new republic was also a turning point in his literary career. The
National Theater was now the cultural center of Czechoslovakia, and Čapek was thoroughly identified with it.

By 1938, however, Hitler had worked up disaffection
among the German-speaking people in the Sudeten-
land, culminating in the infamous Munich Conference
which ceded part of Czechoslovakia to Nazi Germany.
Čapek's death, some of his friends felt, was hastened by
his anti-Nazi activities and his heartbreak over his
ill-fated country.

Čapek was shocked at the catastrophe which human
society could create in the name of progress or idealism.
He connected *R. U. R.*'s theme of the dehumanization
of man as the price of technological civilization, for
example, to the world's increasing trend toward mechanization. Critic S. Moskowitz wrote that "the scientific slaughter of World War I and the efficient mass-
production methods of the United States made a profound impression on Čapek. . . . He did feel that the
idea of scientific progress itself was bad [but he was]
concerned with the use to which new discoveries were
being put and affected lives. . . ."

The same critic reported that, according to Jessie
Mothersale, a close friend of Karel Čapek, the play-

wright got the idea for *R. U. R.* while reading in an automobile. When he suddenly looked out, the "crowds around him seemed to look like artificial beings." This theme of dehumanization, including references to puppets, had been developed by the Čapek brothers in a story called "The System," which appeared in 1908. Furthermore, if we investigate more carefully, we see other suggestions and sources for the play which, incidentally, is also in the tradition of Ambrose Bierce's "Moxon's Master." So far as mechanical beings are concerned, E. T. A. Hoffman had used them in his *Tales of Hoffman.* In the Čapek short story, "L'Eventail," mechanical dolls were involved.

However, the idea of an artificial man, a robot (which derives from the Czech word *robota* for "drudgery, servitude, or forced labor") is traceable to the Hebrew *golem,* meaning "embryo." Čapek was familiar with the Jewish legend of the Golem, the synthetic monster whose home was supposed to have been in Prague. A rabbi, Judah Löw, had supposedly created the Golem from clay in the sixteenth century. The myth was translated into a motion picture in Germany in 1904 and again in 1920 when it was very popular in Czechoslovakia. It is almost certain that Čapek saw the later picture. Even if he did not, the concept of the Golem and robots was current after World War I. In addition, Čapek became more and more interested in the pseudoscientific aspect of literature as is evidenced in the plays he wrote together with his brother, plays such as *The Insect Play, The Makropoulos Secret, Land of Many Names,* and *Adam the Creator.* Employing the Golem concept, *R. U. R.,* of course, is in the best tradition of scientific fantasy even to the detail of having sexless robots (the Golem, too, was sexless) who could not perpetuate themselves.

Yet, Čapek went beyond mere fantasy in *R. U. R.;*
the play is also an implicit sermon. He once explained
in the London *Saturday Review:* "I wished to write a
comedy, partly of science, partly of truth. The old in-
ventor, Mr. Rossum (whose name translated into
English signifies 'Mr. Intellectual' or 'Mr. Brain'), is
a typical representative of the scientific materialism
of the last century. His desire to create an artificial
man—in the chemical and biological, not the mechanical sense—is inspired by a foolish and obstinate wish to
prove God to be unnecessary and absurd. Young Rossum is the modern scientist, untroubled by meta-
physical ideas; scientific experiment is to him the road
to industrial production. He is not concerned to prove,
but to manufacture. . . . Immediately we are in the
grip of industrialism; this terrible machinery must not
stop, for if it does it would destroy the lives of thousands. It must, on the contrary, go faster and faster,
although it destroy in the process thousands and
thousands of other existences. Those who think to
master the industry are themselves mastered by it;
Robots must be produced although they are, or rather
because they are, a war industry. The product of the
human brain has at last escaped from the control of
human hands. This is the comedy of science.

"Now for my other idea, the comedy of truth. The
General Manager Domain, in the play, proves that
technical progress emancipates man from hard manual
labour, and he is quite right. The Tolstoyan Alquist, on
the contrary, believes that technical progress demoral-
izes him, and I think he is right, too. Berman thinks
that industrialism alone is capable of supplying modern
needs; he is right. Emma is instinctively afraid of all
this inhuman machinery, and she is profoundly right.

Finally, the Robots themselves revolt against all these idealists, and, as it appears, they are right, too.

". . . Be these people either Conservatives or Socialists, Yellows or Reds, the most important thing is—and this is the point I wish particularly to stress—that all of them are right in the plain and moral sense of the word. . . . I ask whether it is not possible to see in the present social conflict of the world an analogous struggle between two, three, five equally serious verities and equally generous idealisms? I think it is possible, and this is the most dramatic element in modern civilization, that a human truth is opposed to another truth no less human, ideal against ideal, positive worth against worth no less positive, instead of the struggle being, as we are so often told it is, one between noble truth and vile selfish error."

The play's audiences must have understood much of what Čapek was trying to say. When it opened at the National Theater in Prague on January 25, 1921, it was an instantaneous, popular success, and its author was hailed as Czechoslovakia's leading dramatist. *R. U. R.* got the same reception in Germany. It was then simultaneously produced on October 9, 1922 in London and in New York, where it was the highlight of the theater season and ran for 184 performances. Since then it has been translated and acted in practically every civilized country.

FEATURES OF THE AUTHOR'S STYLE

This edition of *R. U. R.* is a translation from the Czech by Paul Selver. A valid appraisal of the original author's style, therefore, is difficult to make. So much depends on the translator's skill in preserving the author's verbal personality. However, in trying to arrive at an assessment of the writing style of Čapek, who himself frequently translated the works of foreigners for the Czech public and who was scolded for writing for an international audience, we have a few clues to help us in our estimate.

For example, when we realize that a great part of Čapek's literary career was devoted to journalism, we can understand his skill with dialogue. He mingled much with people, had an accurate ear for speech, and could use his experience to produce rapid-fire, humorous lines such as those on pages 18–21M, where Helena Glory is introduced to the staff of Rossum's Universal Robots and mistakes the directors for Robots. Just as effective are the lines on pages 87T–95B, where Helena confesses to the burning of Rossum's formula, and the robots destroy the human beings.

A good journalist tries to be accurate, specific, and authentic. Čapek reveals these traits in different parts of the play. On page 8B, to illustrate, Domain speaks knowledgeably, not glibly, of "catalytics, enzymes, hormones. . . ." Čapek's familiarity with physiological terms, of course, was enhanced by his early training in the life sciences, which he later left for the study of aesthetics. Remember, too, that Čapek was a talented amateur photographer and an art devotee who often "thought" in terms of pictures or tableaux, a talent which is highly desirable in good drama. An instance of such a tableau is Berman's electrocution (p. 93T) on the charged railing with "half a milliard" in bank notes by his side.

Čapek knew the value of juxtaposition—of putting opposites next to each other to intensify contrast. Domain's harsh lines (p. 74T) are immediately softened by his explanation (p. 74M) of why he revolted against poverty and pain. This practice is part of a larger technique in writing, the technique of paradox—of seeming contradiction. Opposing ideas certainly occur often in *R. U. R.* Probably the most obvious one is that, although the Robots bring about a utopian society, in the end this society destroys mankind. Čapek uses a kind of allegory or symbolism throughout the play: the Robots are really men whom technology has dehumanized.

Like a true journalist, Čapek attempts to express "things" and not himself. He was usually successful in doing so since he was an intellectual who dealt with ideas which were his "things" or merchandise. William E. Harkins, who has written a biography of Čapek, reports that he once said: "To understand is my one mania; to express is another. . . . Not to express myself, but to express things. . . . I believe I have succeeded in expressing many things briefly and almost precisely. In my plays I have achieved a certain success by trying to find a real colloquial speech, never a written language. To provide reading matter is a writer's business; for that he is paid, as it were. But to create a living dialogue, to perfect the language, to give full value to human speech, this is a special national and social mission. . . ."

Although Čapek called himself a literary cubist, his work shows some features of expressionism. Expressionism as a literary movement had originated in the German theater in the early 1900's, but it was quickly adopted with some modification by many European dramatists, including Čapek. In *R. U. R.*, we see evidence of expressionism. There is the suggestion of an unnatural atmosphere (the whole picture of a subhuman species running the world); a de-emphasis of the individual (some of the human beings are almost stock figures); a telegraphic kind of dialogue; an almost unreal quality of action; and oversimplification. Nevertheless, *R. U. R.* became a popular play because, in addition to these features of expressionism, it also leaned heavily on realism which made it seem a little more human.

As far as the actual mechanical aspects of writing are concerned, Čapek once confessed: "I work with relative difficulty and with effort. . . . I never enjoy writing, but feel enraged and stubborn, and bite my pen handle. . . ."

"My greatest weakness is a certain inability to concentrate. . . . I plan very little in advance, and my thought is simultaneously its own expression; if I cannot speak or write, I am as dumb as a stump and flighty as a sparrow. . . ."

However, Čapek's considerable literary productions, both with and without his brother's collaboration, are ample refutation of his self-accusation that he was "dumb as a stump," while the depth of his thinking belies the phrase "flighty as a sparrow."

CHARACTER ANALYSIS

Čapek was more interested in ideas than he was in character. Accordingly, in *R. U. R.* he uses his characters more or less heavy-handedly to expostulate his views about modern civilization. The utterances and actions of various managers of the Robot factory are examples of a kind of stereotyping, rather than development of character. Helena, however, seems to have been formed with a lighter touch. She is more emotional, more human than the others in the play, even though she is for the most part a stereotype of femininity. She doesn't only think; she feels. She is petulant and annoyed by Domain's rapid lecture on Robots (p. 8T); she is indignant that the Robotess, Sulla, is not treated like a human being (p. 16M). In fact, having come on behalf of the Humanity League, she is sensitive about the way all Robots are treated: "Robots are just as good as we are," she maintains (p. 15M). She is a missionary and a do-gooder. Yet she repents easily (p. 18M) when she feels sorry for Domain. She feels just as sorry, just as quickly again, for Robots when she learns from Helman (p. 24M) that they have no souls, no love, and no desire to resist. She is honest. She admits that she is a bewildered girl—and a foolish one (p. 28T–M) when Alquist praises "toil and weariness."

Since women are supposed to be intuitive and helpless, according to the stereotype, Helena shows intuition and unreasoned fright (p. 42T–B). Her maid, Emma, calls her a baby (p. 54M) and seems able to influence her mistress as shown on page 89M. This is the same maid whom Helena cannot understand because the woman does not feel sorry for Robots (p.

37M). Helena probably feels a little sorry for herself because she does not have the family for which she longs (p. 42B). However, she is strong willed enough to influence Dr. Gall (p. 78M–B) to give the Robots a soul or sensitivity. Perhaps she is just too disarming with her confessions about her stupidity to which she admits when she says she was a foolish girl. Certainly, her action in burning Rossum's manuscript is not too bright. Concerning this last action, one critic facetiously notes that "man disappears from the earth because Helena cannot mind her own business."

If Helena is simple and emotional, "the eternal woman," then Domain is the "masterly" type. He is very forceful, possessed by a missionary zeal even stronger than Helena's. Domain wants to create a new generation. He hopes that the manufacture of Robots will "shatter the servitude of labor. Of the dreadful and humiliating labor that man had to undergo. The unclean and murderous drudgery" because life was too hard (p. 73M–B). He declaims that he was revolted by poverty and wanted an aristocracy of "unrestricted, free and perfect men" (p. 74M). His utopia would be "nourished by millions of mechanical slaves."

Nevertheless, Domain is a businessman and a realist. He briskly informs his colleagues (p. 59T) that "punctuality's a fine thing. . . . That's what keeps the world in order," and he is interested in profits for the stockholders and envisions increased sales by stimulating, like a munitions maker, nationalistic Robots who will hate and destroy each other. Domain is a man of action, too. He wants quick decisions and gives Helena five minutes to make up her mind about marrying him (p. 30T). Yet, once he is married to her, he is a sincere, loving husband. Even when Helena tells him (p. 89M–B) why she has burned the Rossum manuscript, their supposed insurance, he is forgiving and understanding. He is generally unafraid, strapping on his revolver to fight the Robots (p. 64M). Indeed, Helena admires his constant self-confidence and composure (p. 41B). With it all, he is an honorable man, insistent on keeping his word, even in his dealings with the Robots, censuring Director Berman for Berman's suggestion of deceit. "It's in the interests of humanity to keep to our word," he says (p. 84B).

Perhaps Alquist, the Clerk of the Works, represents the feeling and thinking man, a combination of the emotional and the logical. Čapek called him a Tolstoyan character. He is saved by the Robots because "he works with his hands" as they do (p. 96T). He is humble and creative. He needs work; he is not happy with managerial activity. When he puts on mason's overalls and tells Helena that his "hands are all soiled from work," she tells him (p. 46T), "that's the nicest thing about them." He is "not fond of progress and these newfangled ideas" (p. 47T), and he predicts (p. 48T) that mankind will be destroyed. He prays (p. 47B) for God to "aid mankind to return to their labors." Producing Robots was a mistake, he believes. "There was something good in service and something great in humanity. . . . Virtue in toil and weariness," he claims (p. 28T). He cannot kill others (p. 94M), but he asks the Robots to kill him (p. 96T). He is pessimistic, but logically so, in view of the events which have occurred on the island, and he forecasts sorrowfully that the Robots, too, "will perish without mankind," especially since he cannot create life. However, he does see hope for the future when the Robotess Helena and the Robot Primus seem to emerge as a new Adam and Eve.

Although none of the main characters seems very complicated—and this is due largely to the fact indicated earlier that Čapek was more absorbed in ideas than in behavior traits, unless the traits helped to explain the ideas—some comment might be made of the lesser division chiefs, such as Physiologist Dr. Gall, Chief Engineer Fabry, and Managing Director Berman. The Managing Director, despite his title, appears to have the soul of a petty clerk. When the Robots threaten the human beings, he continues with his ledgers. Nothing seems to matter except that the accounting work be up to date. "Let me go on with my bookkeeping," he pleads with Domain (p. 72B). Again (pp. 81B–82T), he lectures Helena on business procedures and then concludes: ". . . when I drew up these balance sheets, it entered my mind that history is not made by great dreams, but by petty needs of all honest, moderately knavish, and self-seeking folk. . . ." In brief, he means everybody in general. This is the credo by which he lives.

The mechanistic, intolerant Chief Engineer Fabry sees life from a more technological position than does Berman. He scorns human engineering and believes that human machines are imperfect. "From a technical point of view" he says on page 23M, "the whole of childhood is a sheer stupidity." If he is reasonable in his attitude toward Robots, it is only because he doesn't like "damaged articles."

In Dr. Gall, we find an apparently cynical attitude toward Robots. Although he himself is discerning enough to detect a varying sensitivity in different Robots and to understand the source of the sensitivity, he shrugs mentally and says that nothing can be done about the situation since "all the manufacturers in the world are ordering Robots like mad" (p. 53M). In a cool understatement (p. 65B), he estimates the strength of the rebellious Robots, and (p. 77M) sagaciously explains that they have "ceased to be machines." Yet he was "human" and scientific enough to experiment with them, to infuse into them a human quality. Nevertheless, he is honest enough to accept responsibility for having done so and thereby precipitating the destruction of the human beings on the island.

Čapek's readers have observed that he uses nonhuman characters like robots, puppets, and insects because he is somewhat distrustful of the human personality. He dislikes social conformism with its loss of personal identity. William E. Harkins, for example, suggests that this attitude on the part of Čapek is the reason why his characters seem cold and lifeless. He tried not to get involved in deep characterizations of human beings. Yet this situation in itself is paradoxical because Čapek constantly tried to make a better life for mankind; he was passionately concerned about the fate of humanity.

CRITICAL EXCERPTS

Selected from the criticism written about Karel Čapek, here are some excerpts that should prove challenging to you. We have included page references to *R. U. R.*, indicated in parentheses, so that you can review sample passages to help you decide whether to accept or reject the quoted comments.

1. *Čapek's civilized cosmopolitanism [is] admirable for a play of ideas such as* R. U. R. . . .

The Nation, June 11, 1930.

It is important to set forth this opinion at the outset of an evaluation because Čapek wrote the play with the overriding purpose of satirizing the machine age; consequently, some critics are willing to overlook the fact that it is not an example of a polished art form.

Kenneth Macgowan commented:

2. *In* R. U. R. *there is plot and action . . . but the keynote is still satire . . . a satire on capitalism. . . .* R. U. R. *is full of much that is inconsistent and its atmosphere is curiously repulsive. Yet it remains fascinating and novel in its materials, and in the third act the revolution is certainly effective to a high degree.*

Theater Arts, Volume 7, 1923.

Oliver Elton continued this idea, emphasizing that Čapek's plays:

3. *. . . satirize the social order and depict, often in symbolic form, the perils that threaten it with shipwreck. . . . [The satires'] wealth of ideas, their strengths of purposes, and their pertinence today, must be recognized. And yet, considered as works of art, they have perils of their own. They*

*are full of faults and fissures which will hardly stand close
analysis and which are easily passed over in the theatre.*

> *Essays and Addresses,* Oliver Elton,
> Edward Arnold & Co., 1939.

4. *It* [R. U. R.] *is arresting satire. Mr. Čapek does not
reveal, however, the genius of the true satirist—the power
of continually shocking and surprising the reader or the
spectator, the genius of relentless revelation of human weakness and stupidity.*

> *The Independent,* November 25,
> 1922.

An interesting sidelight reminds us of the timeliness
of the satire or message in the play. Note that the play's
theme was most timely in the aftermath of World War
I. Critic Elton refers to the pertinence of the play in
1939. In 1922, the play was also considered timely.

5. *To the present-day civilization, rent and torn, and ob-
sessed with a fear of its own destruction, the play speaks
with terrific force. It could speak more briefly and, in consequence, more pointedly. Even in its discursiveness, it is a
great drama written in a vividly imaginative way.*

> *New York Evening Telegram,* Octo-
> ber 10, 1922.

Is the play still timely? Is mankind headed toward
an "aristocracy of the world? An aristocracy nourished
by millions of mechanical slaves? Unrestricted, free,
and perfect men" as Domain hopes (p. 74M)?

Notice that Macgowan's comment in 2 above mentioned inconsistency in *R. U. R.* In appraising the justice or injustice of this charge, decide, for example,
how to reconcile Čapek's devotion of most of the play
to the destruction of both the human beings and the
Robots and then the sudden switch in the Epilogue
to the creation of a rosy dawn with a new Adam and

Eve (pp. 110–115). The *New York Evening Telegram*
drama critic thought, in his review of October 10, 1922,
that the play should have ended after the third act
because the Epilogue was a letdown to an otherwise
stirring drama. Furthermore, concerning the matter of
inconsistency, William E. Harkins, Čapek's biographer,
points out that in general Čapek "does not really believe that machines will destroy man, or that modern
technology will robotize him." He explains:

6. *Paradox of philosophical ideas is an important trait in
Čapek's writing. This follows from the conflicts within the
author himself, as well as from the intrinsic ambiguities of
ideas and symbols. In* R. U. R. *machines bring utopia, but
in the end destroy man.*

Karel Čapek, William E. Harkins,
Columbia University Press, 1962.

The same biographer observes that in *R. U. R.* the
formula creates more Robots, but in the end Robots
become men. Is this an inconsistency or a logical development? Did you have difficulty accepting the
premises implicit in pages 7–17? The author of the
following passage apparently did not have difficulty:

7. *Unlike the works of the "cult" mongers, this play has
no need of subtle explanations. It explains itself. It is* . . .
*"thoughtful"; it is even dramatic, and it is, even in its stag-
nant moments, quite interesting.*

The New York American, October
10, 1922.

Yet, elsewhere in the same review, the above critic
said: "The play begins as an extraordinarily searching
study of the nature of human life and human society
and ends in a marshmallow bog." The "marshmallow
bog" may be part of the structural weakness which

critics find in the turnabout mentioned earlier in this discussion—the Adam and Eve theme revealed on pages 113T–115. Do you regard this section as a weakness? If you do, perhaps Čapek's biographer can explain why the canons of playwriting seem abused. "Since the end of the play is the miracle of life, the transformation of Robots into men . . . Čapek was right to introduce this philosophical note to his play. . . . The threat to man's existence can be meaningful only if the spectator really grasps that man is about to pass from the earth, if he comprehends what a 'great thing' it was 'to be a man.' " (Note the similarity of the last phrase to Alquist's statement on page 28T.)

How do you feel about the ending? Should the play have been arranged more conventionally? Is Act III too anticlimactic, is it necessary as it stands, or is it "good theater"? Does *R. U. R.* forecast too much in Act III? Is the Epilogue a letdown from pages 112–115? Or do you agree with Heywood Broun that "these excesses do not seem . . . to mitigate against the theory that Čapek is potentially one of the great men in modern drama"?

Generally considered, if you agree that the strengths of the play are greater than its weaknesses, you may be interested in the reactions of the following critics to the first performance of *R. U. R.* at the Garrick Theater in New York City on the night of October 9, 1922.

8. . . . *This fantastic composition, even if it is somewhat indebted to the ideas of authors so far apart as Mary Shelley, Hauptmann, and Lord Dunsany, is, in form at least, a veritable novelty, full of brains and of purpose. . . .*

J. Ranken Towse in *The New York Evening Post,* October 10, 1922.

9. *In the intelligence of its writing, the novelty of its action*

and the provocative nature of its mood, R. U. R. sustains the high tradition of the Theatre Guild.

John Corben in *The New York Times*, October 10, 1922.

10. . . . *Like the H. G. Wells of an earlier day, the dramatist frees his imagination and lets it soar away without restraint and his audience is only too delighted to go along on a trip that exceeds even Jules Verne's wildest dreams. The Guild has put the theatregoers in its debt this season. R. U. R. is super-melodrama—the melodrama of action plus idea, a combination that is rarely seen on our stage.*

The New York Evening Sun, October 10, 1922.

Is it likely that the last critic, an authority on Čapek, has judged him accurately?

11. . . . *Karel Čapek is an extremely ambitious and subtle practiser [sic] of the craft of fiction, a philosopher-poet passionately interested in the problems of truth and justice, in short, a great artist who has to be reckoned with as one of the major figures of contemporary literature.*

René Wellek in the *Slavonic Review*, Volume XV, 1936–1937.

The opinion of a middle-of-the-road critic would probably be that, despite the play's drawbacks, it has withstood many critical attacks very successfully and that, as S. Moskowitz, author of *Explorers of the Infinite*, reminds us, "with the possible exception of Rostand's *Cyrano de Bergerac* and Molnar's *Liliom*, [*R. U. R.*] is the most frequently anthologized of modern European plays in English translation." Although inclusion in collections is not necessarily proof of a play's quality, it does give an indication of breadth of appeal.